A Catholic and Hands-On Appro

Behold and See 2

More Science with Josh and Hanna

by Nancy Nicholson

with Mary Piecynski

For Little Folks

Consultant:

Mary Piecynski holds a Bachelors in Biology, received teacher's certification, and is completing her Master's thesis in Education. Mary has sixteen years of experience homeschooling, in addition to teaching science and other subjects for several years in both elementary and secondary grades. She currently tutors science at the university level. Mary, her husband Tom, and family reside in rural Ohio.

Illustrations:

AnneMarie Johnson

Photos:

Credits may be found on page 154.

ISBN: 978-0-9824585-9-4

Printed by Sheridan Books, Inc.
Chelsea, Michigan
May 2011
Print code:

For Little Folks
P.O. Box 571
Dresden, OH 43821
www.forlittlefolks.com

Distributed by
Catholic Heritage Curricula
P.O. Box 579090, Modesto, CA 95357
1-800-490-7713 *www.chcweb.com*

For more titles by Nancy Nicholson, visit www.chcweb.com!

Dedicated to
Our Creator God,

Maker of man, Who from Thy throne
Dost order all things, God alone;
By Whose decree the teeming earth
To reptile and to beast gave birth.

—from *Hominis superne Conditor*,
attributed to Pope St. Gregory I, 6th century

Table of Contents

Please note: Although every effort has been made to ensure the safety of all experiments within this book, users are responsible for taking appropriate safety measures and supervising children during experiments. Catholic Heritage Curricula disclaims all responsibility for any injury or risk which is incurred as a result of the use of any of the material in this book.

Introduction and Instructions

As children begin to discover the astounding world that God created, they at the same time begin to uncover the mysteries of science. Rather than being at odds, these two discoveries issue from one and the same Source.

This Catholic science text presents to the child both Creation and Creator, in a context familiar to the child: the family.

To present the lesson, please read it with the child.

Reading ability varies widely at this developmental level. Some children will be able to read the pages independently; others will require a good deal of teacher assistance. Depending on the ability of the child, some may read alternate sentences with the teacher reading the remainder, or the teacher may choose to read the entire lesson to the child.

To ensure that an informed discussion of the material ensues, activity pages should always be read by the teacher or with teacher assistance, even if the child is an advanced reader.

Just as importantly, all hands-on activities require the assistance of the teacher, both for safety reasons, and also to ensure that the activity's purpose is presented effectively.

In addition, lessons progress more smoothly if all supplies are available. Please check lessons at least a week in advance to ascertain that activity items are on hand.

Hands-on activities reinforce and bring lessons to life. Encourage the child to use the scientific method of observing, comparing, grouping, and measuring change as much as possible in these activities. Most of all, encourage questions about and exploration of God's astounding Creation!

Preface

On Josh and Hanna's farm, juicy apples hang from apple trees. Fuzzy yellow chicks scratch in the barnyard. In the summer, God sends warm rains to water the fields; sparkling snow blankets the farm in the winter. All around them, Josh and Hanna see God's beautiful world.

Josh and Hanna study these and other marvels of God's Creation. They learn about living things, like plants and animals that live in deep oceans. They learn about non-living things, like melting rocks and erupting mountains; they also learn how things work.

Learning about science helps people think of new ways and new machines to make our lives better, and to serve Jesus in others.

When Josh grows up, he wants to find ways to grow more food to feed the poor around the world. And Hanna wants to become a missionary doctor! Josh and Hanna like to study science.

Josh and Hanna even "use" science when they play, and so do you! Do you know how?

Let's find out!

God works throughout all activity after the manner of all these three causes, final, efficient, and formal. First, He is end, aim, purpose ... Second, He is efficient cause ... All things act by God's power, and He, therefore, is the efficient cause of all activity ... Third ... the formal cause ... He is the cause, not merely as providing the active form ... but also as sustaining the form and power of everything.

—St. Thomas Aquinas, *Summa Theologica* 1, 105, 5

Simple Machines, Work, and Energy

Josh Uses Tools

"WHAT happened to your hair?" Mother stared at Josh as he slid into his chair for morning prayers.

Josh's hand flew to his head. "Um, I guess I forgot to comb it."

"Back upstairs, then," Dad pointed. "And don't forget to use your tools," Dad winked at Josh.

"My tools?" Josh was puzzled. "What do you mean?"

"Your tools," Dad smiled, "like we talked about in science yesterday."

"You mean hammers and saws?" Josh said. "I remember that tools like hammers and saws make it easier to build

things, but I don't use them to fix my hair!"

Dad laughed. "No, I hope not. But not all tools are used for building things. In fact, you use tools every day, even if you are not a builder.

"A comb is also a tool. Tools are things that make our work easier.

"A comb is a tool that makes it easier to fix your hair. But a tool will not do work by itself," Dad added. "Tools need something or someone to make them work."

"I will put my comb to work right now. If I ever have to comb my hair with a saw," Josh laughed, "I will ask Mom to shave my head."

Tools at Work

Tools are things that make work easier.

Saws, scissors, and knives are used for cutting. Saws, scissors, and knives are tools that make work easier.

If you did not have a shovel, how would you dig a hole? If you did not have a broom, how would you sweep crumbs from the floor?

Shovels and brooms are tools that make work easier.

Directions: Circle the things that are tools.

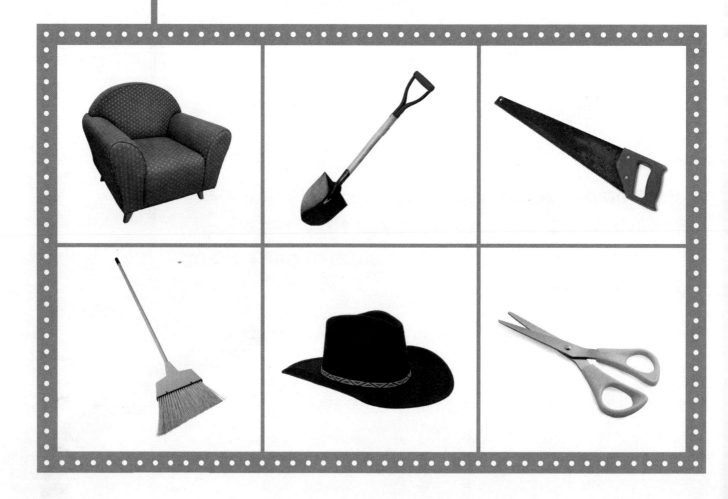

Inclined Plane

Simple machines and tools make work easier. An inclined plane is a simple machine. Inclined planes make it easier to move things from a low place to a higher place.

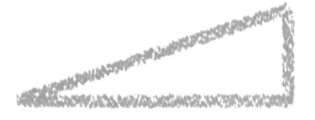

Maybe you have seen pictures of the pyramids in Egypt. Pyramids were built long, long ago. There were no big trucks or big machines to help. How did the Egyptians lift the huge stones to the top of the pyramids?

Some think that the Egyptians used ramps to move the stones. The stones would be too heavy to lift straight up, all at once. But ramps let us move things from a lower place to a higher place a little bit at a time.

Ramps are inclined planes. Things can be pushed and dragged from a lower place to a higher place on ramps and inclined planes.

Stairs make an inclined plane. The ramp on a delivery truck is an inclined plane.

Inclined planes also make it easier to move things faster from a high place to a low place. A slide is an inclined plane. A hill is an inclined plane that makes sleds go fast from top to bottom!

Lever

A lever is another tool or simple machine. You probably have levers in your house, and maybe even in your backyard!

A lever makes it easier to lift heavy things. Under the lever is a *fulcrum* (FUHL-kruhm). Pushing down on one end of the lever lifts the heavy load on the other end.

Teeter-totters are a type of lever. Did you know that you are strong enough to lift your dad? You can, if you use a teeter-totter lever.

This is how it is done: Move the fulcrum so that the lever is longer on one side of the fulcrum, and shorter on the other side.

Now put the heavy load on the short end of the lever, and push down (or sit down) on the long side of the lever. If your dad is the "heavy load," and you are the weight pushing on the long end, you can lift your dad!

(If you cannot move the lever or the fulcrum on your teeter-totter, you can move the load. That is, your dad can move forward on the teeter-totter, so that he is closer to the fulcrum.)

A claw hammer is another type of lever. Have you ever tried to pry, or lift, a nail out of a piece of wood, without using a hammer? (Prying is a type of lifting.) It is much easier to pry the nail out with the right tool, isn't it?

The head of the hammer acts like a fulcrum, and the handle of the hammer acts like a lever. When the hammer handle is pulled, the nail pops out!

Scissors are two levers joined at the fulcrum. Pliers and nutcrackers are also types of levers. Even the pull-top ring on some cans is a type of lever, used to pry open the can!

How do you use levers and inclined planes in your work and play? How many can you find around your house?

Tools and Simple Machines
at Work and Play

Directions: Draw lines to show which are levers and which are inclined planes.

lever

lever

lever

inclined plane

inclined plane

inclined plane

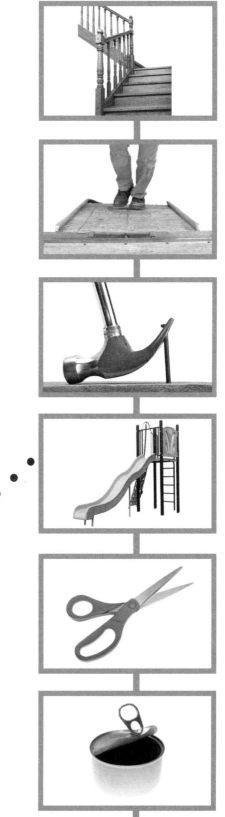

Simple Machines

Observe and Compare

In science, we can look and see, or observe. We observe that some things are alike. We observe that some things are different. When we look to see how things are the same and how they are different, we compare.

Today we will do some experiments with levers. We can observe and compare.

Lever Activity #1: Observe and Compare Levers

Supplies

lever: ruler or similar sized piece of wood or metal

load: 12 coins of equal value and two identical lids from milk or juice jugs

fulcrum: cylindrical spice jar

duct tape

Directions:

Lay the spice jar on its side on a counter or desk; tape securely. Make sure lids are dry inside, then attach a three-inch long piece of duct tape to the lid by pressing the middle of the tape firmly into the center inside of the lid. (This creates a depression so that the coins will fit inside.) There should be enough tape hanging over on each side to attach the lid to the lever. Now securely tape one lid at each end of the lever.

Place the lever on the fulcrum, with the fulcrum at the center. Put two coins in each lid.

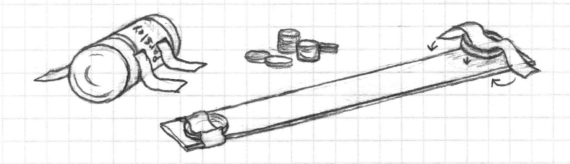

Observe and Compare:

When the fulcrum is exactly in the center of the lever, and the load on each end is exactly the same weight, is the load balanced?

Now add two more coins to one lid only. What happens to the lever when the load is heavier at one end than at the other?

Next, move the lever so that the fulcrum is much closer to the heavier load. What happens when the fulcrum is moved closer to the heavier load?

Now allow the child to experiment with different numbers of coins on each side of the lever, and with different fulcrum positions.

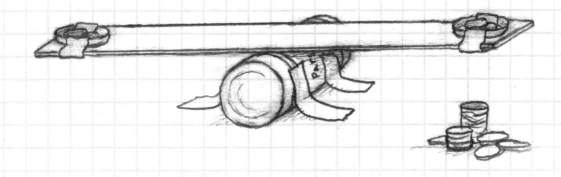

Lever Activity #2

Directions:

Direct the child to attempt lifting the selected piece of furniture without assistance.

Now stick the lever under the edge of the furniture. (Center the lever so the furniture doesn't slide sideways during lifting.) Place the fulcrum under the opposite end of the lever, about a foot away from its end. (In other words, the lever should be much longer on the furniture side than on the "pushing" side.)

Direct the child to push down on the "short" end of the lever.

Did the lever lift the furniture?

Now move the fulcrum to the midway point between the lever's free end and the furniture; direct the child to push down on the free end.

Did the lever lift the furniture?

Now move the fulcrum so that it is only about eight inches from the furniture and direct the child to push down on the free end.

Did the lever lift the furniture?

Compare the different attempts. How did moving the fulcrum affect the ability of the lever to lift the furniture? Was it easier to lift the furniture with or without the lever?

Levers help lift heavy things, making our work easier.

Supplies

lever: broom, mop, or other tool with *heavy* wooden handle

fulcrum: possibilities include wooden block at least 3"x3"x6" or larger; 29 oz. or larger fruit can, unopened (This activity will dent the can significantly, so be prepared to have fruit for dinner.)

load: living room chair or other furniture that is too large for child to lift unaided (furniture should have a space under at least one side to enable lifting)

14

Simple Machines

Inclined Planes

Supplies

box of books that is too heavy for child to lift

long board or boards wide enough to make ramp for box

low table or chair

Directions:

Set the lower end of the ramp against a wall, so it doesn't move. Position the low table or chair so that the ramp reaches the top of the table or chair.

Fill the box with enough books that the child can push the box, but not lift it easily.

Set the box at the bottom of the ramp and direct the child to push the box to the top of the ramp and onto the table or chair.

Observe and compare: Was it easier to move the box without the ramp, or with the ramp?

Now, if the box is too heavy to lift from the table, remember that inclined planes not only help move things up; they help move things down, too!

Inclined planes help lift heavy things, making our work easier.

Wedge

A wedge is a simple machine that helps cut or push things apart. Wedges are thin or pointed on one side and thicker or wider on the other.

Knives and axes are wedges that are thin on one side and thicker on the other. These tools can cut or split things apart.

Nails, tacks, and needles are wedges, too. Nails, tacks, and needles are pointed on one end and thicker on the other end. (A sharpened pencil is a wedge, too!) These wedges push things apart.

16

When a tack is pushed into a wall, the sharp end "pushes" the wall apart enough for the tack to stick. Think of how hard it would be to make the flat end of the tack go into the wall!

Your front teeth are wedges, too! They are thinner on the biting edge, but are wider where they meet the gums. These special wedges make it easier for you to "cut" your food into bites when you eat.

The front of a boat or ship is also a wedge. This wedge shape "cuts" into the waves to make the boat travel more smoothly and quickly through the water.

A shovel is a special kind of wedge; it is both a wedge and a lever. The edge of the shovel is a wedge, which makes the shovel push apart the ground more easily. The handle of the shovel makes a lever, so dirt is easier to lift from a hole.

Screw

Screws are simple machines, too. Screws have "threads" that go around a center "pole." These threads are actually an inclined plane that goes around and around the pole!

Some screws are called bolts; bolts have a flat end. Other screws have a pointed end. The pointed end is a wedge that makes it easier for the screw to go into wood or metal.

Screws can fasten things together, but there are other kinds of screws, too. A spiral staircase is a type of screw! The end of a light bulb is a screw, and so is the top of a bottle with a screw-on bottle cap.

The end of a drill is called a "bit." The bit is a type of screw, too.

Wheel

Another simple machine is the wheel. Like all simple machines, wheels make our work much easier.

What do you think would happen if your brother or sister sat inside a box, and you had to push the box along the sidewalk? It would not be easy, would it?

Now think how much easier it would be to push that box if it were on wheels. Why, I'll bet you have done this many times before. If you have a wagon, you have a box on wheels!

How many indoor and outdoor toys do you have with wheels on them? Quick! Go count them, and print the number here: _____.

Now, how many of these toys would work just as well without wheels?

Like all other tools, wheels make our work and play easier. But tools will not work by themselves. They need someone or something to make them work, to power them.

Some machines, like cars and lawn mowers, are powered with gas. Some are powered with wind or water power. Others, like shovels and skateboards and wagons—and combs—are powered by a person like you. That is, the tool or machine can be very helpful, but it will not be any help at all unless you use it.

Our Holy Faith is a little like this. Jesus gave us His Church, filled with "holy tools" to make our lives happier in Him, and to help us reach Heaven more easily.

Some of these "tools" are the Sacraments of Penance and Holy Communion, Holy Scriptures, and the holy Sacrifice of the Mass itself. But these tools cannot help us if we don't go near them. Let us "pick up" these wonderful tools from Jesus, and use them to help us reach Heaven!

Find the Wedges and Screws

Circle the wedges.
Put an X on the screws.

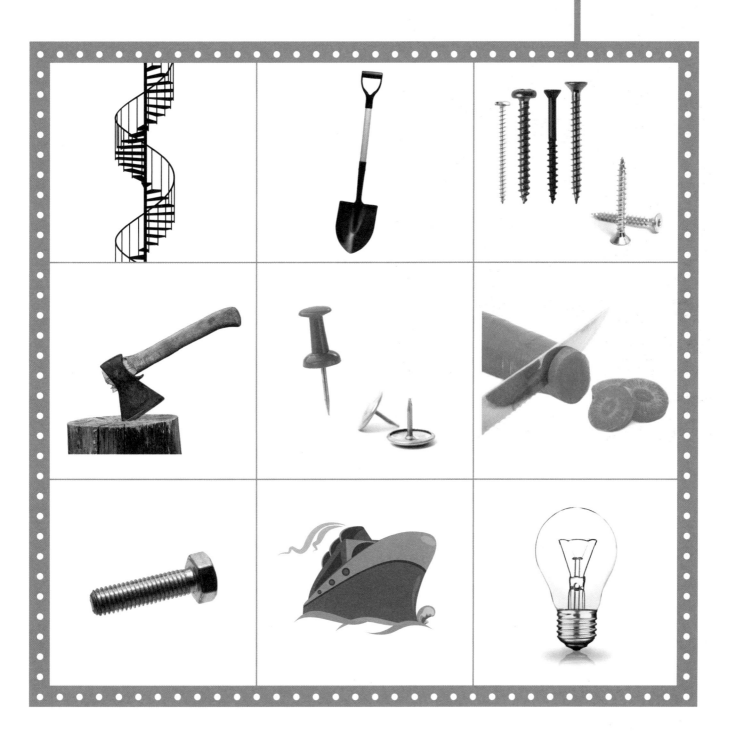

Simple Machines

Wedges

Directions: Begin with the tack and piece of cardboard. Turn the tack over so that the sharp side is up. Using the thimble, try to push the tack into the cardboard.

Did the tack go into the cardboard? Why or why not?

Now turn the tack over and push it into the cardboard, pointed end first.

Did the tack go into the cardboard? Why or why not?

The pointed end of the tack is a type of wedge that "splits" or pushes the cardboard apart to make room for the "stem" of the tack.

Now turn the nail pointed end up, and try to hammer it into the piece of wood. Then turn the nail over and try with the pointed end down. Which way does the nail go into the wood the most easily?

Now push the screw, pointed end first, into the cardboard. Try the same thing with the bolt. Did the screw go into the cardboard more easily than the bolt? Why or why not?

Would it be hard to build a house with nails that had flat ends, without a wedge shape? How do wedges make our work easier?

Supplies

nail

tack

screw with pointed end

bolt

hammer

piece of wood

thimble

piece of thick cardboard

Simple Machines

Wheels

Directions: Set the board on a carpeted floor. (Carpet teaches the lesson more dramatically; if there is no carpeted floor available, bare flooring will still work.) Tell the rider that he is going to be a "load" for the board to carry. Direct him to place one foot on the board and try to "skateboard" across the floor.

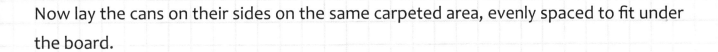

How well did the board carry its "load" across the floor?

Now lay the cans on their sides on the same carpeted area, evenly spaced to fit under the board.

Lay the board on top of the cans. Direct the "rider" to stand *next* to the board, with a person on either side. Direct the "rider" to take the hand of the person to his right and to his left. The "rider" may now place one foot on the "skateboard" and "skate."

Did the "skateboard" move more easily with the cans underneath? Why?

The cans acted as wheels under the board. Wheels are simple machines that help carry loads. Wheels make our work—and play—easier.

What Is Work?

"Push harder!" Hanna grunted to Josh. "I am tired of stubbing my toe on this old rock every time we walk to the pond." Hanna strained with all her might as she bent over the big rock in the path.

"I'm pushing as hard as I can, but it just won't budge!" Josh stopped to wipe sweat from his forehead. "Stubborn old rock. Dad said we could move it, but it's just too heavy."

Hanna looked down the path toward the house. "Hey, Dad is coming to help. He has some kind of long stick with him."

"That's not a stick," Josh laughed, "it's a crowbar. I think I know how Dad is going to help."

"How are my best workers?" Dad called as he came near. "It looks like you've been working, yet no work has been done."

"You could say that," Hanna nodded as she brushed dirt off the front of her jumper. "Ugh. We lifted, and pulled, and pushed, and nothing happened."

"So as much effort as you put in, no work happened," Dad said.

"In science, we say that *work happens when force moves something from one spot to another*," he explained. "Lifting, pulling, and pushing are all types of force that can move things.

"But not all force is work. Sometimes force is used but nothing moves. If nothing moves, no work is done," Dad went on.

"You both tried very hard to make the rock move, but it wouldn't budge. So, while you tried your best, no 'work' was done because the rock did not move a distance.

"Work is what happens when force makes something move."

"I think this will help." Dad handed the crowbar to Hanna. "This makes a good lever. You can push the end of the crowbar into the ground next to the rock. Then Josh can push down on the other end."

Hanna worked the crowbar into the soft ground next to the stubborn rock. "OK, Josh! You can push down now. I want to see this rock move!"

As Josh pushed down on the crowbar, the rock began to come out of the ground! Josh pushed the end of the crowbar again, and the rock rolled off the path!

"Wow, Dad, this lever did what we couldn't do." Josh waved the crowbar over his head like a flag of victory.

"Yes, and now we can say that work happened, because the rock was moved from one place to another. You two make a good team!" Dad praised.

What Is Energy?

"...Father, and of the Son, and of the Holy Spirit, Amen!" Hanna crossed herself. "I'm starved! Moving that rock was hard work."

"Yup," Josh agreed. "I don't think I have a bit of energy left. Please pass some of that people fuel."

"People fuel?" Hanna asked. "I thought those were sandwiches."

Mom laughed as she passed the sandwiches to Josh. "Fuel is another word for stored energy. Energy is the power that makes something do work.

"People and animals can push and pull and lift because of the energy they get from food. Food is stored in your body and used as 'fuel' to power whatever work you do."

"That's right," Dad added. "Machines need power to do work, too. Machines use stored energy from fuels like gas and coal. Energy from the sun and wind can power machines, too."

"Like the windmill Grandpa had on the farm when he was a boy," Josh commented. "I remember he said that the wind powered the windmill. When the windmill turned, it brought water up from the well."

27

"Yes, and newer windmills are used for power today, too," Dad agreed. "Water is also used for power."

"Oh, like when we visited Uncle Russ and Aunt Maureen!" Hanna remembered. "They took us to see the dam that had *turbines* (TOOR-baynz) inside.

"Aunt Maureen said the water came through the dam and made the turbines spin around and around. The spinning turned water power into electric power."

"That's right, Hanna," Dad said. "God gave us many ways to make all the energy we need."

Kinetic and Potential Energy

Energy is the power that makes something do work.

Food energy gives power to your muscles so you can jump and run and do work. Gas energy is the power that moves your car.

If your car is parked in the garage, the gas energy isn't being used. When the car is parked in the garage, we say that the gas energy is *potential* (poe-TEN-shul) energy. Potential energy is energy that could possibly be used, but isn't being used now.

When the car is started and backed out of the garage, the potential energy is put to work. Energy at work is called *kinetic* (kuh-NEH-tick) energy. (*Kinetic* comes from a Greek word that means "move.")

When Josh and Hanna moved the rock on the path, kinetic energy was at work. Kinetic energy is moving energy.

Potential energy | **Kinetic energy**

Have you ever blown up a balloon and then let it loose to fly around the room? When the balloon flies, kinetic energy is at work. What if you blew up the balloon, but tied it instead? The "wind energy" inside the balloon would be *potential* energy, energy that wasn't being used, but was waiting to be put to use.

Water behind a dam, waiting to flow into turbines and turn them, is potential energy. When the water is allowed to flow into the turbines and turn them, kinetic energy is at work.

Have you ever made a line of dominoes, and then pushed the first one in the line? What happened to the rest of the dominoes in the line?

Before the first domino is pushed, it has potential energy to knock over the dominoes, but no energy is being used when the dominoes are at rest. When the first domino falls, kinetic energy is at work, setting in motion the falling of the rest of the dominoes in the line.

A "resting" rubber band has potential energy. When the rubber band is pulled back, it shoots across the room. Kinetic energy is at work.

You can make a bowling set with plastic glasses and a softball. Set the glasses up like bowling pins on a floor with no carpet. Stand ten steps from the glasses and roll the ball toward them. Kinetic energy is at work in the rolling ball. When the ball knocks over the glasses, kinetic energy is at work, too.

Sitting at the top of the slide is another example of potential energy. Sliding down is an example of kinetic energy.

Kinetic energy is moving energy. Potential energy is energy that could possibly be used, but isn't.

If you have dominoes, a balloon, a rubber band, or a softball and plastic glasses, you can experiment with potential and kinetic energy.

Kinetic and Potential Energy

Circle the things that show kinetic energy.
Put an X on things that show potential energy.

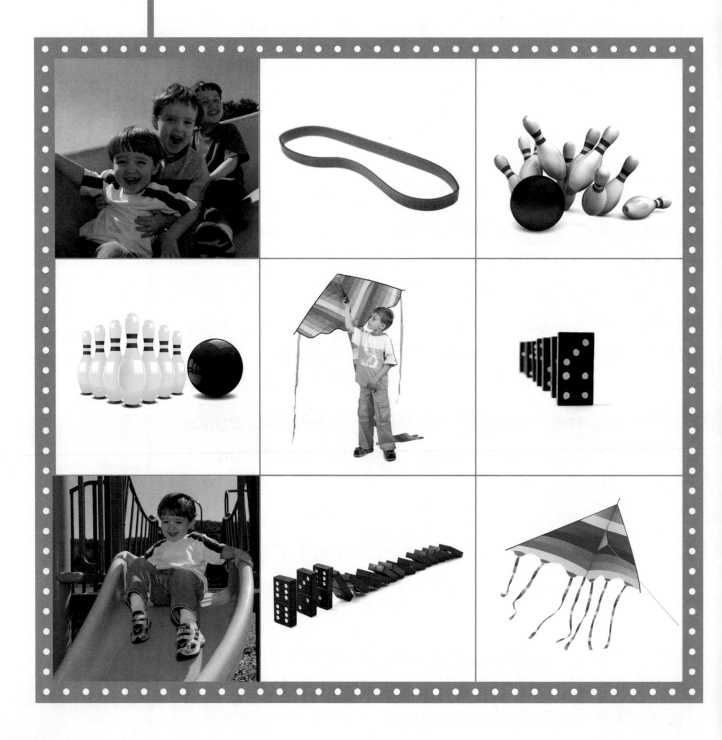

Simple Machines Make Energy

Long ago, waterwheels were used to make energy. This energy was used to power different kinds of machines.

Josh and Hanna's great-great grandfather lived on a farm that grew corn and wheat. The corn and wheat were taken to a nearby mill. At the mill, a waterwheel powered the machines that ground the wheat and corn into flour.

Let's make a very simple waterwheel, to pull a small car!

Supplies

two large, sturdy, round paper plates

4 disposable drinking cups (bathroom size, ideally, but larger cups can be cut down to size)

dental floss or thin string

empty spool or bobbin

stapler

small toy car

thin dowel at least 12" long

tape

1.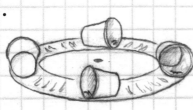

2.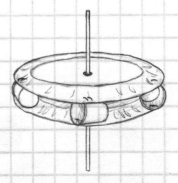

Directions:

Find and mark the center of the first plate. Set the second plate under the first, and punch a hole through both centers, so the holes match up.

Staple the cups, evenly spaced, to the bottom of the first plate. *The opening to all cups must face the same direction.* Turn the first plate over, so the cups are facing up.

Set the second plate on top of the cups and staple the cups to the second plate.

3.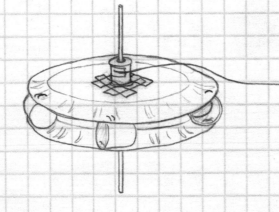

Stick the dowel through the center holes of both plates, so the dowel is the same length on both sides of the plates.

4.

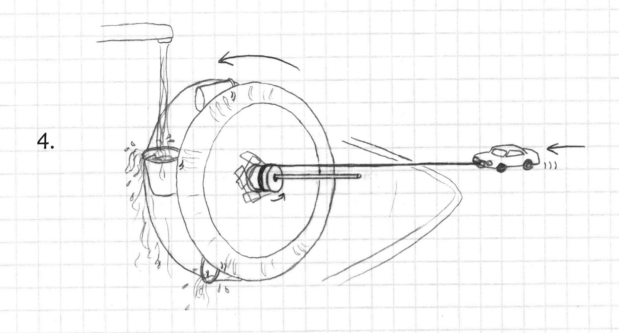

Slip the bobbin or spool over the dowel on one side of the plate. Securely tape the bobbin or spool to the plate. (Be careful not to get tape over the end of the spool where the dowel comes out; the plate should be able to rotate freely around the dowel.)

Cut a three-foot long piece of floss or string. Tie one end to the car; securely tape the other end to the spool.

Set the car on the kitchen counter, about two and a half feet from the sink.

Grasp the waterwheel by the dowel; hold under the sink's spigot and turn the water on gently, so the cups fill and the wheel turns. The turning wheel will cause the string to wind around the spool, pulling the car along with it.

Moving water can provide energy to do work.

GOD PROVIDES WATER FOR THE WORLD THAT HE CREATED

God Provides Water
for the World that He Created

How is water used in your house? Think of some of the ways, then write them here.

_____

_____

_____

_____

_____

Everyone in the world needs water to drink, to cook with, to bathe, and to wash clothes. Water is used to make crops grow, and even to make power to run machines.

What would we do without water? Will the world ever run out of water?

No, thanks be to God's good designs.

Did you know that most of the world is covered with water? If all the oceans and lakes and rivers were put together, and all the land put together into one grand island, it might look a little bit like this:

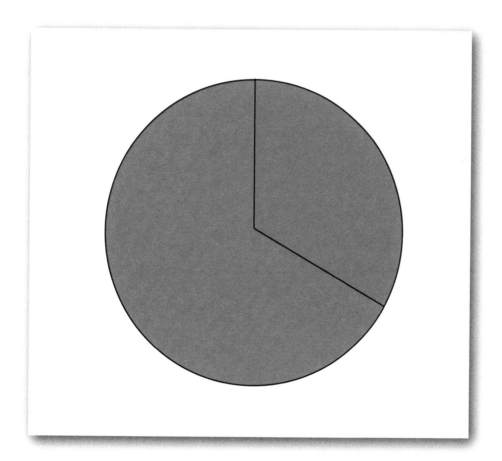

That's a lot of water, isn't it? On top of that, God made a way for that water to "rise" from the lakes and rivers and oceans, and fall on places where there are no lakes and rivers and oceans!

First, sunlight warms the water in the oceans and on land. This makes some of the water *evaporate* (ee-VAP-uhr-ate), or change from liquid water into "water gas" that you cannot see.

Now, don't be confused! "Gas from water" is not the gas that is used in cars. Did you know that there are many kinds of gas? The air you breathe is made up of different kinds of gases, too. But the gas we are talking about is "gas from water."

Second, this "gas from water" goes into the air and begins to turn into clouds. High in the sky, the clouds begin to get cold.

Then comes the *third* step: In the colder air, the "water gas" begins to *condense* (kuhn-DENSS), or turn back into liquid water.

You can maybe guess what happens in the *fourth* step: the water starts to drip from the clouds and fall to the earth. The rain falls on towns and cities and farmers' fields. The water makes its way to little creeks and bigger creeks and rivers and lakes and to the ocean.

It looks a little bit like this:

And then the sunlight warms the water, and the "water-making" starts all over again. Isn't God smart to know how to keep His world watered, forever?

Now, some places in the world have lots of water, while other places are very dry. It makes sense for people who live in dry places to *conserve* (kuhn-SIRV), or use water wisely. But in God's good plan, the world will never run out of water.

Which Happens First?

Directions:

Oops! Somebody mixed up the steps that make liquid water turn into "water gas" and then back to liquid water again. Can you figure it out?

Figure out the first step. Then put the steps in order by correctly numbering them 1, 2, 3, 4.

_____In the colder air, the "water gas" begins to condense, or turn back to liquid water.

_____Sunlight warms the water. This makes some of the water evaporate.

_____Water starts to drip from the clouds and fall to the earth.

_____This "gas from water" goes into the air and begins to turn into clouds.

Evaporation and Condensation

Observe, Measure, Compare

You can make water evaporate, or turn into gas.

You can make water condense, or turn from a gas to liquid water.

Directions:

Help the student carefully measure one cup of water and pour it into the uncovered pan. Bring the water to a vigorous boil. Boil the water for two minutes.

Show the student that the inside of the lid is dry, then turn the burner off and place the lid on the pan. Wait one minute, then uncover the pan.

Supplies

2 or 3 qt. saucepan with *dry* lid

glass or metal measuring cup (glass is best)

What is on the inside of the lid? How did the water get from the pan to the lid?

Now carefully pour the water in the pan back into the measuring cup. Is the water level the same as it was before boiling? Where did the missing water go?

Heat turns liquid water into a gas, which rises into the air. (The water evaporated.) When the gas cools, it returns to its liquid state. (The water condensed.) The water from the pan rose into the air in "clouds" of steam. Some of the "water gas" was captured by the lid and condensed there.

Natural Resources

God's Gifts to Man

Conservation and Wise Use

To "conserve" means to use what we have carefully and wisely, without wasting it. But conservation does not mean never using something.

When God created the Heavens and the Earth, He made man above all other created things. Then He gave man dominion over all creation (Gen.1:28-29). This means that mankind was to rule over everything on the Earth, to care for it, and wisely use what God created for man's use.

Let's imagine that there was a huge pitcher full of grape juice in the refrigerator. Imagine that you were thirsty, and your mom said you could have some juice.

Would you drink the whole pitcher full? I hope not! You would be responsible and drink a wise amount.

At the same time, do you think your mom would put a whole pitcher of grape juice in the refrigerator, and then never let anyone drink the juice?

No, that would not be wise use, either. Not to use what God has given us is not wise use. It is not use at all.

God blessed the Earth with rich gifts of water, and soil. He has blessed us with precious rocks and metals, trees and plants and animals.

Let us thank God for these good gifts and use them wisely, to our benefit and His glory.

What Are Natural Resources?

"Are you ready for a treasure hunt?" Dad asked.

"Yippee!" Josh squealed. "Where are we going? Do I need a shovel and pail? Did pirates once live around here?"

"Nope." Dad shook his head. "No pirates. All you need are pencil and paper. We're going to 'treasure hunt' some *natural resources*. (NAT-choor-uhl REE-sore-sez)."

"What do natural resources look like?" asked Hanna. "I don't know what they are."

"Natural resources are all the treasures that God created in His world for our use," explained Dad. "Man cannot make natural resources, but he can use these gifts from God in many ways.

"Oil, gas, and coal are natural resources found inside the Earth. These natural resources fuel our cars and machines and help heat and light our homes. Trees, plants, and animals on land and in the ocean are natural resources. Water, soils, and rocks are natural resources."

"Rocks are a natural resource?" Hanna was surprised. "We don't eat rocks or use them to power machines. How are rocks a natural resource?"

"There are many different kinds of rocks," Dad answered, "and they are used for different things. Metals for cars and kitchen pans and jewelry all come from rocks. Rocks and *minerals* (MIHN-ir-uhlz) are in and under the soil. They are mined or dug from the earth for our use.

"In fact, you use minerals every day. You even eat minerals."

"Not me," Hanna shook her head. "I don't eat rocks."

"When you salt your food," Dad smiled, "you are eating a mineral. When you look through the window, you are looking through glass made from the minerals in sand. Minerals are all around us."

"You said trees are a natural resource," Josh offered. "I remember Uncle Russ talking about the trees he cares for as a forester, and how the trees are used.

"He told me that the wood for our house and furniture and paper and cardboard all came from trees. And he said we don't need to worry about running out of trees any more than we need to worry about running out of corn.

"Uncle Russ said that we plant and harvest corn, and he plants and harvests trees."

"So he's a tree farmer," Hanna added. "And he told me he even takes care of sick trees, to keep the forests well. So he's like a tree doctor, too."

"That's right," Dad agreed. "He checks the forests to see how the trees are growing, and if any have been attacked by insects that will kill the trees. Those trees can be cut and taken out of the forest.

"Insects can move from tree to tree and kill a whole forest. Cutting the 'sick' trees saves the healthy trees. Dead trees also mean forest fires, burning dead trees and healthy trees alike.

"But wood from 'sick' trees can still be used, if they are cut in time. Good foresters help keep the forest healthy, and make sure nothing is wasted. They even care for the soil."

"Mom told me that miners care for the soil, too," Josh offered.

"Yes, miners dig into the ground to take out coal and salt and rocks that have minerals in them. When they are done mining, they put the soil back in place so plants will grow there again.

"Your mother grew up near a

coal mine. When the miners were done mining the coal, they put the soil back in place. Then they planted trees and other plants.

"By the time your mother was all grown up, grass and woods grew where the mine once was. Deer and other animals now live there, because miners know how to care for the Earth, too.

"Trees, rocks, and minerals are all good gifts that God gave for our use. And today we are going to 'treasure hunt' all the natural resources that we find around us."

"I've got my 'shovel and pail'!" Josh said as he waved his pencil and paper. "Let's start digging!"

Natural Resources All Around

Directions: You can have a natural resources "treasure hunt," too. Find things made from trees, oil, rocks, and minerals. List what you find in the proper columns.

Here are some ideas to get you started:

ROCK, METAL, MINERALS	COAL AND OIL	TREES
jewelry	plastic products	houses
bikes	bike tires	furniture
talc powder	dishes	paper
concrete	vitamins	cardboard
bricks	lip gloss	egg cartons
furniture	soap	vanilla flavoring
nails	crayons	books
pans	carpet	gum
glass	vinyl flooring	pencils

Find the Natural Resources

God created our natural resources. Man *uses and makes* things from these natural resources, but man cannot make the natural resources themselves.

Circle the natural resources that God created.

Thinking about Natural Resources

Look around your bedroom. It is probably filled with things that were given to you by your parents or other people: a bed, sheets, blankets, clothing, toys, a crucifix.

But those things all started as natural resources. The sheets, blankets, and clothing probably came from plants that God created, like cotton, and perhaps some fabric made from oil.

The toys are made from metals and plastics and wood. All of these are, or come from, natural resources, created by God for a good purpose and to His glory.

How many things do you see that you yourself made?

But what are these things made of? Do you see that everything man owns began at the creation of the world? In a way, nothing on Earth belongs to us; we simply use and care for that which God has made. "A Christian is a steward of the Lord's goods." (*Catechism of the Catholic Church #952*)

You, too, were created for a good purpose, by a loving Father.

We care for all that God has created for our use, but all that is in or on the Earth will pass away one day. How much more important that we also care for the precious gift of life that He has given to us and to all mankind, for He made us to live forever.

Let us thank and bless God for all that He has given us! (See Daniel 3:35-65.)

DIRT!

Soil Is a Natural Resource

When you come inside from play, I'll bet you wash the dirt from your hands. Perhaps sometimes you help do the washing, to clean the dirt from your clothes. Maybe you even sweep dirt from the floor as one of your chores.

Yet, did you ever think what might happen if all the dirt in the world disappeared?

Dirt, or soil, helps catch and hold rainwater, sort of like a sponge. The dirt soaks up the rainwater so it doesn't quickly run off into creeks and rivers. Then the water in the soil can be used by plants, and animals, and people.

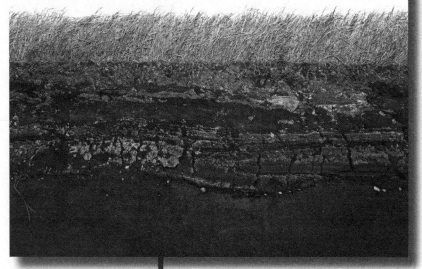

Of course, plants grow in the dirt, too. These plants feed animals and people. Where there is no dirt, plants cannot grow. Dirt is a pretty important natural resource, don't you think?

Most dirt is made up of three kinds of soil: sand, silt, and clay.

If the soil where you live is mostly sand, you might know that water runs through it quickly. Since sand dries out quickly, plants growing in the sand can become dry quickly, too.

Clay soil is almost the opposite of sandy soil. When clay is dry, it is almost solid like a brick. It is hard for roots to grow in dry clay. When clay is watered, it can hold so much water that plants may get soggy.

Silt holds water better than sand does, but not as much as clay soil. Silt has more "plant food" in it than sand or clay, and is better for gardening than

soils that are mostly sand or mostly clay.

When these three soils are mixed well, they make *loam*, which is the very best type of soil for growing plants. What kind of soil do you have where you live?

Erosion

The Yellow River, in China, gets its name from the yellowish dirt that chokes its waters. The river flows through an area where wind and rains have washed the soil away for thousands of years.

Some kinds of soil blow away easily. And soil can wash away in heavy floods, if the soil is not protected. When soil blows or washes away, we say that the soil has *eroded* (ee-RODE-ed).

Erosion (ee-ROE-zhun) carries soil away. If enough soil is carried away by erosion, plants can no longer grow in that place.

Ocean waves can erode the land next to beaches. Flooded rivers wash dirt away from riverbanks. Heavy rains can "scour" unprotected dirt and wash it into rivers. This dirt then muddies the rivers and kills some of the fish in them.

Blowing dirt, carried by the wind, can turn into choking dust storms. Sometimes the wind-carried dust can bury and kill growing plants.

Plants cannot grow where the soil has washed or blown away. Where soil has eroded, farmers cannot grow food and God's children go hungry. How can erosion be stopped?

Conservation of Soil: Stopping Erosion

The best way to stop erosion is to keep it from starting in the first place. Wise use and planting grasses and trees can conserve the soil.

When plants cover the soil, wind cannot blow the soil away. Roots hold trees and grasses in the soil; these roots also hold the soil in place so rain and flooding cannot easily wash it away. Planting special grasses and trees can help make new soil in time, but it is much better to stop erosion before it begins.

Many years ago, parts of North America suffered wind storms that caused terrible erosion. Soil blew away and many people lost their farms. These places were said to be part of the "Dust Bowl."

Tree planting and careful use of the land "repaired" the soil in those places. Today, some of the best farms in North America grow crops in what used to be the "Dust Bowl."

Everything that God created has a reason and a purpose, even the natural resource that we call dirt. We can care for the soil so there is no erosion. We can "repair" land that has been eroded, so crops can be grown again. And we can thank God for His gift of dirt!

"Dig Up" the Correct Word

Directions: Pick the correct word from the box to fit in each blank line.

eroded   sand   dirt

clay   repair   loam

1. Plants cannot grow where there is no _____.

2. This kind of soil dries out quickly. _____

3. When this kind of soil dries, it is almost like a brick. _____

4. When sand, silt, and clay are mixed well, they make _____, which is the best kind of soil for growing plants.

5. When soils blow or wash away, we say that the soils have _____.

6. Tree planting and careful use of the land can _____ soil that has eroded.

Soil in My Yard

Observe and Compare: Activity #1

Directions:

To begin the hole, dig out a shallow circle of grass, or turf, about 15" in diameter. Set this circle of turf aside for later replanting.

Continue to dig the hole to a depth of about 12". Observe the soil. Is the dirt at the top of the hole a different color or texture from the dirt near the bottom of the hole?

Supplies

trowel or small shovel

bucket or small plastic bowl with a little water

empty plastic jar with lid

Pick up some of the dirt from the bottom of the hole. Sprinkle some water on the dirt and try to roll the dirt into a ball. If you can make a ball, does the ball stay together well, or does it crumble?

- Soil that is gritty and won't form a ball at all is **sandy**.

- Soil that holds together a little bit, but crumbles easily and feels smooth and sort of soapy is probably **silty**.

- Soil that forms a ball like clay and feels sticky is probably **clay**!

- **Loam** is a mixture of all three of these soils.

Activity #2

Now fill the jar about half full of dirt, taking samples from both the bottom and top of the hole.

Fill the jar almost to the top with water. Put the lid on, and shake the jar well, to mix the dirt and water. Then let the jar sit, undisturbed, for at least four hours.

Observe and compare:

After four or more hours, look at the layers in the jar.

Grains of sand are heavier than the rest of the soil, and will settle to become the bottom layer. Silt is the next layer, with clay at the top. (Clay is much lighter than sand, so it floats to the top of the jar.)

Is your soil mostly sand, or mostly silt, or mostly clay? Or, do you have loamy soil that has a good balance of sand, silt, and clay?

You may also notice small bits of old leaves and plants in your jar. These bits, called humus, help enrich your soil so that plants will grow better.

Let your jar sit overnight. Did the soil continue to settle? (Soil may be returned to the hole, which will be used again in the next activity.)

Soil that contains a lot of sand warms quickly in the spring, so seeds can be planted earlier than in clay. Because sandy soil is loose, it is good for growing root crops like carrots, beets, parsnips, potatoes, radishes, and onions. Asparagus also likes sandy soils.

Soil that contains a lot of clay stays cool much longer than sandy soil. Plants that like cooler weather, like peas and lettuce, often grow better in clay soils. Cabbage also grows well in clay soils. Clay is a "heavy" soil. Root crops like carrots and beets do not grow as well in clay soils; it is difficult for them to break through the heavy clay.

Most plants grow best in silty or loamy soils.

If you have room in your yard for a small garden, what kind of vegetables would you like to plant?

Erosion

Activity #1

Directions: (This activity is to be done outdoors.)

In this activity, observe what happens when unprotected dirt is exposed to "flooding."

Half-fill the baking pan with dirt from the hole used in the last activity. Press *lightly* on the dirt to compact it somewhat. Set the pan next to the hole, with one end over the edge of the hole.

Set one end of the pan on a board, or rocks, so that the pan is tilted toward the hole and water can run off into the hole. Now slowly pour the pitcher full of water onto the dirt at the "top" end of the pan.

Supplies

non-clay soil

baking pan, at least 9" x 13"

trowel

2 qt. pitcher of water

Observe and compare:

What happened to the dirt when water flowed over it? Now pour a pitcher of water onto grass-covered soil. Did the dirt wash away? Why or why not?

Branches, leaves, and grass reduce the impact of water falling on the soil. Roots from plants hold the dirt in place, but soil that is exposed easily erodes. Replanting exposed soils helps prevent erosion and soil loss.

Now you can refill the hole and "replant" or replace the turf that was removed to create the hole.

Activity #2: Field Trip!

Visit a lake, river, creek, or the seashore where there are exposed banks.

Observe and compare:

Walk along the edge of the body of water, if possible. Look for trees, bushes, or grass growing on top of the bank, with roots extending down the side of the bank.

Now look for areas with less vegetation on and above the banks.

Compare the two areas. Does the bank with numerous plants and roots jut farther out toward the body of water than the less protected bank? What role have the plants above and the roots below played in slowing erosion?

Perhaps there are highway "cuts" next to roads that you travel. How has erosion been controlled on those cuts? Have areas that weren't replanted, or were replanted poorly, eroded? What steps might be taken to stop the erosion?

THE EARTH ON

WHICH WE LIVE

The Earth on Which We Live

We have learned about different kinds of soils, which we sometimes call dirt. Another word that also means dirt is *earth*.

When we capitalize this word, Earth, the meaning changes a little. *Earth* is the name of our world, the planet on which we live.

Do you ever wonder what is under the "earth" of the Earth? What lies below the soil under our feet? Let's find out!

Have you ever eaten a raw plum? The outside of a plum is covered with skin, isn't it? Juicy fruit is under the skin, and at the very center of the plum is a "plum stone," or pit.

The Earth is a little bit like the plum, with three basic layers. The Earth's first layer is called the *crust*. The crust is a little like a "skin" of rock and dirt covering the outside of the planet. Mountains make up the "taller" parts of the crust.

Lower parts of the crust make up the "floor" of the seas and oceans. The oceans "sit" on top of the crust

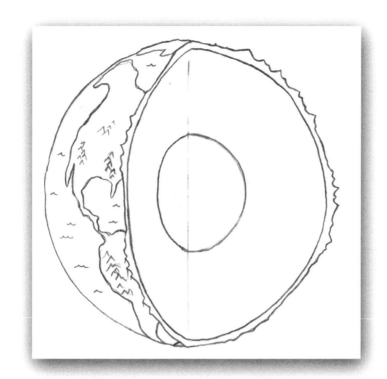

below them, a little like mud puddles. Mud puddles are water that has filled "low places" in the ground. The oceans fill "low places" in the Earth's crust.

The second basic layer of the Earth is called the *mantle*. The mantle is made of very hot rock. The mantle is mostly solid, but lava that has "poured out" of a volcano came from inside the Earth's mantle, too.

The third basic layer, at the center of the Earth, is the *core*. The core is solid at the center, but liquid rock on the outside. The core is the very hottest of the Earth's layers.

We live on and see only the Earth's crust. But as the skin is only a thin layer on the outside of a plum, the crust we live on makes up only a small part of our planet. Together, the crust, mantle, and core make up the layers of the Earth on which we live.

Layers of the Earth

Color and label the layers of the Earth.

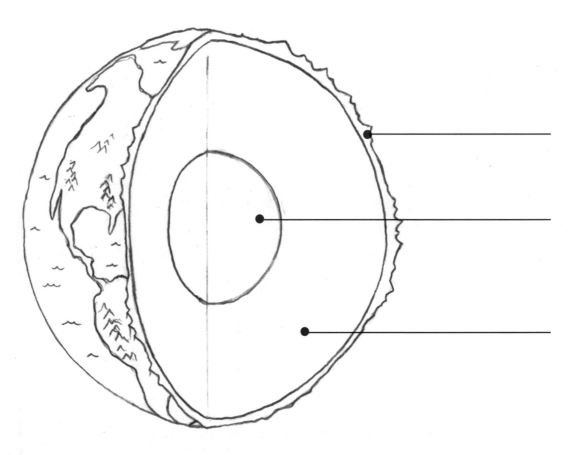

Directions: Pick the correct word from the box to fit in each blank line.

crust   mantle   core

1. the very hot center of the Earth _____

2. the Earth's layer on which we live _____

3. the second layer of Earth _____

Modeling Layers of the Earth

"Half a Globe" Ice Cream Model

Supplies

two different colors/flavors of ice cream, 1/2 gallon each

chocolate "shell" ice cream topping (the type that hardens into a firm coating when it contacts the ice cream)

rounded bowl large enough to hold 1/2 gallon ice cream

about 1/2 c. blue frosting to represent bodies of water

1/4 c. chocolate chips to represent mountain ranges

Directions: Please read all directions before beginning this activity.

Soften the ice cream that will be used to create the "mantle." Spoon the ice cream into the bowl so it is level with the top of the bowl. Press firmly so there are no empty spaces. Smooth the top, then scoop out a round indentation at the very center.

Fill the indentation, which will "model" the Earth's core, with the second ice cream and smooth again so the top is flat. Then return the ice cream to the freezer for at least three hours, until it is frozen hard.

Set the bowl on the counter for several minutes, just long enough for the ice cream to begin to soften at the edges, so it will release easily from the bowl. Invert the ice cream over a large plate and remove the bowl.

Quickly press or scoop out indentations, about half an inch deep, on the surface of the ice cream to represent lakes and oceans. Return the ice cream to the freezer for an hour, to harden again.

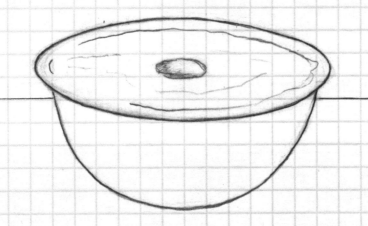

Remove the ice cream from the freezer and quickly squeeze and spread the chocolate topping over the ice cream "half globe." Quickly stick chocolate chips into rows to create mountain ranges. When the topping has hardened, fill the indentations with blue frosting.

The chocolate shell on the "half globe" represents the Earth's crust and soil; the frosting represents the bodies of water that sit upon the crust. Chocolate chips represent mountain ranges jutting from the Earth's crust. Inner layers of ice cream represent the mantle and core.

To serve: (THIS STEP IS FOR ADULTS ONLY!!)

Dip the blade of a large, sharp knife into hot water. Gently cut through the "crust" to create slices that include each of the layers.

Different Kinds of Rock

Just as there are different kinds of soil, there are different kinds of rock, too. Perhaps you have seen smooth, white stone floors that look very different from the gravel in your driveway or on a park path.

Why are the rocks so different from one another? It is because the rocks are formed in different ways.

Sedimentary Rock

Sediment (SAID-uh-muhnt) means "to settle." Sedimentary rock is formed from tiny bits of sand, silt, and other broken-up rocks, like this:

Once there was a bubbling river, with a pebble-covered beach at its edge.

Erosion from floods and wind had carried tiny bits of rock, or silt and sand, into the river and onto the beach.

One spring day, there was a terrific rainstorm. The river rose and flooded the pebbled beach with more silt and sand.

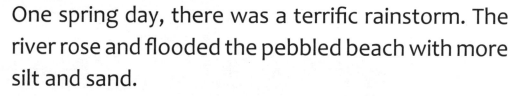

The flood waters mixed silt and sand with the pebbles.

After a while, the flood stopped, and the river shrank away from the beach. Now the beach with its mixed pebbles and sand and silt dried out.

That summer, wind erosion blew dirt and sand across the beach.

When fall came, leaves drifted onto the sand and pebbles and silt.

After a very long time, so many heavy layers of silt and sand and pebbles *settled* around the river that the lowest layers were pushed tightly together into a mixed rock. This rock is called a *conglomerate* (kahn-GLOM-ehr-uht).

A conglomerate is just one kind of sedimentary rock. *Sandstone* is a sedimentary rock formed when layers and layers of sand settle over one another, pressing the bottom layers into hard, sandy rock.

Sandstone

When layers and layers of mud and clay are pressed together, they become *shale.*

Limestone is a sedimentary rock mostly made of shells! This stone is used in road-building, and also to make concrete and cement. Can you guess why limestone is often found near oceans, or where oceans once were?

Shale

Conglomerates, sandstone, shale, and limestone are all sedimentary rocks, formed layer by layer over a long period of time.

Limestone

If you live near an ocean or river, you can probably find sedimentary rock nearby. You may even have some of this rock in your house or garden!

Metamorphic Rock

Slate roofing

Michelangelo's "Moses"

Metamorphic (meht-uh-MORE-fik) means "to change form." Sedimentary rock forms when layers and layers of silt, mud, sand, or shells press down on layers below. But what happens when the layers at the bottom are already rock, like shale?

Weight and heat from so many layers and layers of rock above can change shale into a rock called *slate*. This stone is used to make roofing, flooring, and walkways.

Limestone can also change over time, into a beautiful rock called *marble*. Marble is a metamorphic, or changed, rock used in buildings, for floors, and even for carving into statues.

Perhaps your church has a marble altar for the Sacrifice of the Holy Mass!

Igneous Rock

Igneous (IGG-knee-us) means "from fire." Can you guess how igneous rock is made? If you guessed that it started out very hot, you are right!

Igneous rock starts underground, in the mantle of the Earth, as extremely hot, liquid rock called *magma* (MAG-muh). *Granite* forms from magma that cools slowly underground. It is used to make buildings because it is strong and will last for a long, long time.

Granite

Sometimes, magma pushes up to the surface of the Earth and starts to flow from a mountain called a *volcano* (vahl-KAY-noh). Magma that comes out of the Earth is given a new name: *lava* (LAH-vuh).

Lava

When this hot, liquid rock called lava cools, it becomes hard. Some lava hardens into a rock that looks like shiny black glass. At other times, lava comes out all bubbly and foamy, a little like thick shampoo suds. When this lava cools, it becomes a hard "foamy" rock called *pumice* (PUH-miss). Pumice is so full of air bubbles that it floats!

Pumice

If you live near volcanic mountains, you may have seen igneous rock used on roads and park pathways.

What kind of rocks can you find where you live? Are the rocks mostly sedimentary, metamorphic, or igneous?

"Matching" Rocks

Directions: The information on the left tells about words on the right. Draw lines from the words on the left to the words that "match" on the right.

1. sedimentary rock made from shells   igneous

2. This "rocky" word means "changed form."   magma

3. This "rocky" word means "from fire."   pumice

4. hot liquid rock   sandstone

5. This "foamy" rock comes from a volcano.   limestone

6. sedimentary rock made from sand   metamorphic

Making "Sedimentary Rock"

Supplies

1/4 c. water

1/4 c. butter or margarine

1 tsp. vanilla

(Mix in a saucepan and heat to melt butter; set aside.)

1 c. graham cracker crumbs, divided 3/4 c. in one bowl and 1/4 c. in another bowl

1 c. chopped nuts in separate bowl

1 c. raisins in separate bowl

3 c. powdered sugar

3 T. cocoa powder

(Stir these together in a bowl and set aside.)

1/4 c. flaked coconut

9" x 13" pan

Directions:

Today we are going to make a treat that is a little like sedimentary rock.

Once there was a bubbling river, with a pebble-covered beach at its edge. (Put the raisins and nuts, representing pebbles, into a 9" x 13" pan.)

Erosion from floods and wind had carried silt and sand into the river and onto the beach. (Add cocoa powder and powdered sugar mix, followed by 3/4 c. graham cracker "sand.")

One spring day, there was a terrific rainstorm. The river rose and flooded the pebbled beach. (Pour the water and melted butter mixture onto the contents of the pan.)

The flood waters mixed silt and sand with the pebbles. (Gently stir the mixture together until the crumbs and powdered sugar are well blended into the mix.)

After a while, the flood stopped, and the river shrank away from the beach. Now the beach with its mixed pebbles and sand and silt dried out.

That summer, wind erosion blew dirt and sand across the beach. (Sprinkle 1/4 c. graham cracker crumbs on top.)

When fall came, leaves drifted onto the sand and pebbles and silt. (Sprinkle coconut on top.)

In time, there were so many heavy layers of silt and sand and pebbles that the bottom layers were pushed tightly together into a mixed rock called a conglomerate. (Pat down and refrigerate for 1 hour before serving.)

81

Minerals

Most rocks are made of a mix of *minerals* (MINN-uh-ruhlz), although some are made of just one mineral. Because the minerals are usually mixed together in the rock, it can be hard to tell which minerals the rock is made of just by looking at the rock.

Looking at a stack of blueberry pancakes, you might not know that, besides blueberries, they also contain eggs, milk, flour, and butter. After all those ingredients are mixed together and cooked, you can't easily see them in the pancakes. The mixture of minerals inside rocks is a little like this.

Scientists who study rocks have tests that they use to help them find out which minerals make up a rock. One test is called a *streak test*. A streak test is made by scratching the rock against a special kind of tile.

Talc

You might be surprised to learn that a green rock can make a white streak, or a black rock can make a red streak. The mineral talc, or soapstone, can be white, green, or brown, but it makes a white streak.

Talc is mined almost all over the world, including Australia, the United States, the United Kingdom, and in Canada. Are there any talc mines where you live?

Another way to find out what minerals a rock is made of is the *scratch test.* The scratch test tells the hardness of the rock.

Quartz

Talc is a very soft rock, a "1" on the hardness scale. It is so soft that you can easily scratch it with a fingernail, and break it between your fingers.

Quartz, on the other hand, is a "7" on the hardness scale. Diamonds, "10" on the scale, are the hardest of all the minerals. Quartz and diamonds cannot be scratched with a fingernail, a penny, or a nail. But quartz and diamonds can scratch other things, like steel and glass.

Diamond

Quartz is found in rocks all over the world. Quartz is clear, somewhat like glass. It is often colorless, but it can also be pink or smoky in color. Can you find rocks with quartz in them where you live?

Feldspar

Another very common mineral is feldspar. Feldspars look a little like quartz, but they are usually cloudy, not clear like quartz.

Hematite

Magnetite

Minerals can be metals, too. Soils or sedimentary rocks with streaks of red, yellow, or orange probably have iron in them. Hematite is an "iron mineral"; it is usually pink or reddish in color. Hematite makes a reddish streak in a streak test.

Magnetite is another "iron mineral." Have you ever visited a river's edge or beach that had "ribbons" of black sand? You may have been seeing fine pieces of magnetite.

If you live near a river or beach with black sand, take a magnet along the next time you visit. If the sand contains magnetite, the pieces of magnetite will jump to the magnet.

There are more than two thousand different minerals on our Earth! Different colors and shiny, sparkling, or dull spots in and on rocks give hints about the minerals present in them. Examine rocks where you live; what types of minerals do you think they contain?

(A *Field Guide to North American Rocks and Minerals*, or similar rock and mineral identification book, can help you identify your rocks.)

Rock Formations Field Trip and Collecting Rocks

What kind of rocks are found where you live? How were these rocks formed? You can visit rock formations where you live, or make an "internet visit."

Directions:

Locating rock formations in your area is easy! Internet search "geologic formations" + the name of your state or province. This will bring up a list of various geologic formations, often in parks, in your vicinity. You might be surprised at the number of excellent examples of sedimentary, metamorphic, and igneous rock formations in your area.

Supplies

Field Guide to North American Rocks and Minerals or similar rock and mineral identification book

magnifying glass

Be sure to take a magnifying glass and a good field guide along on your field trip.

If at all possible, please make this a hands-on field trip. However, if you cannot get out in the field, the internet also has excellent international "virtual field trips." Search "virtual geology field trips," "geology link + virtual field trips," or "virtual geology field trips for classrooms." "Visit" Australia's sandstone Ayers Rock; the limestone cliffs of Dover, England; sedimentary formations of the Grand Canyon; and igneous formations from Asia to Alaska.

The next activity involves rock classification and identification. Whether from your yard, or from a field trip, please collect several samples.

My Discoveries: Rock Formations Field Trip

Rock and Mineral Identification: Observe and Compare

On my field trip, I visited: (name of actual or virtual location)

_____

_____

On my field trip, most of the rock was: (sedimentary, metamorphic, or igneous)

_____

_____

If the rocks are sedimentary, can you see layers in your rock?

If the rocks are igneous, can you see bubbles in the rock, or do some of the rocks look as if they were melted before hardening?

Use a magnifying glass to observe and compare the rocks you have discovered.

Ayers Rock, Australia

White Cliffs of Dover, England

Grand Canyon, Arizona

What differences do you see?

Do some of them sparkle? Sparkling rocks may contain quartz.

If the rock looks "pearly," it may contain talc.

If your rock is shiny, it may contain minerals that are metals.

Try a streak test on a concrete sidewalk or other hard surface. What colors do your rocks leave behind? (This test won't be completely accurate, but will demonstrate that the minerals in rock may contain colors different from the sidewalk.)

Can you scratch the rock with your fingernail, or with a penny, or a nail? Is the rock hard, or soft?

Can you find rocks that look like yours in a field guide? If so, print their names here:

_____

_____

_____

_____

(If you'd like to learn more about streak tests and minerals, online search "streak color common minerals.")

Volcanoes: New Rocks and New Land

"Mom! Dad! We got a letter from Sr. Mary of the Nativity in the Philippines!" Hanna burst through the screen door, waving the mail in her hand. "Her newsletter has a picture of a big volcano on the front!"

"Thanks for getting the mail, Hanna," Dad said as Hanna handed him the newsletter. "She had planned to visit Mt. Pinatubo on a mission trip. There's our daughter, right next to the mountain." Dad proudly showed the picture of Sr. Mary to Mom and Josh.

"I hope she made it home before it erupted," Josh worried. "If I lived in the Philippines, I wouldn't want to live near a volcano."

Dad smiled. "Josh, if you lived in the Philippines, you

would have to live near a volcano. Much like Hawaii, the islands that make up the Philippines are formed from volcanoes.

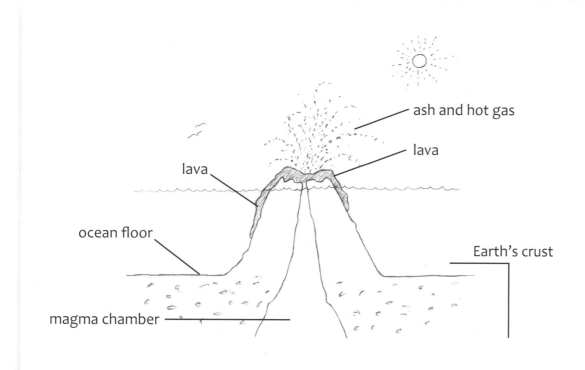

"The volcanoes started below the crust of the Earth. Hot magma pushed upward and came out of the mountain as lava. Lava cooled and hardened into rock. Then more hot lava poured out on top of the first layers of rock. The volcanoes rose upward, unseen mountains growing under the ocean.

"In time, the erupting volcanoes grew so tall that their tops became islands in the ocean. Like the Kilauea Volcano in Hawaii today, the lava spread farther and farther, making more and more land as the volcano erupted."

"What's erupted?" Hanna asked.

"When ash, hot gas, and lava pour or burst from volcanoes, we say they *erupt* (ee-RUHPT)," Mom answered. "The eruptions that created the beautiful islands of Hawaii and the Philippines are part of God's good plans for His Earth. The lava makes new land, and the ash becomes rich soil for farms.

"But Sr. Mary didn't have to worry about Pinatubo erupting during her visit," Mom pointed out. "Scientists watch the mountain so they can warn people before an eruption."

"Uncle Russ told me about a volcano erupting when he worked in Alaska," Josh offered. "Mt. Redoubt

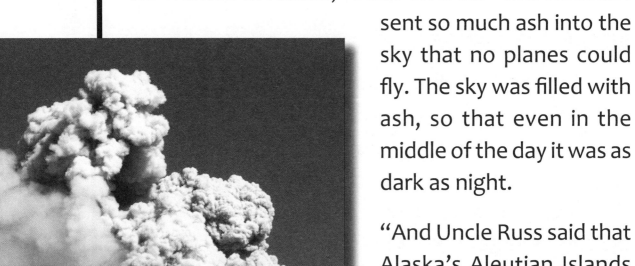

sent so much ash into the sky that no planes could fly. The sky was filled with ash, so that even in the middle of the day it was as dark as night.

"And Uncle Russ said that Alaska's Aleutian Islands were volcanoes, too, but most of them are *dormant* (DOOR-muhnt), kind of like they are sleeping."

"Yes, we say that an erupting volcano is *active*," Dad explained. "A volcano that is dormant has been active, and could be active again at some time.

"Some volcanoes are *extinct* (ecks-TINKT). Extinct means the volcano was active long ago, but will never again erupt. Dormant volcanoes, on the other hand, could erupt again.

"Scientists *monitor* (MAHN-uh-tur), or watch and measure changes in the mountain. This helps them know when a dormant volcano will become active again."

Hanna looked thoughtful. "Living things like people and plants and animals grow and change. I always thought that things like rocks and mountains would not change.

"But mud can change to sedimentary rock, and sedimentary rock can change to metamorphic rock. Mountains can grow and change, too.

"Is there anything that doesn't change?" Hanna asked.

"Yes," Dad smiled. "Jesus Christ is the same yesterday, today, and forever. God's faithfulness, His love and mercy toward us, His truths, will never change." (See Heb. 13:8; Ps. 100:5; Jer. 31:3.)

Land-building Volcanoes

Use words from the Word Bank to label the picture.

One word is used twice.

When you finish the labels, color the picture!

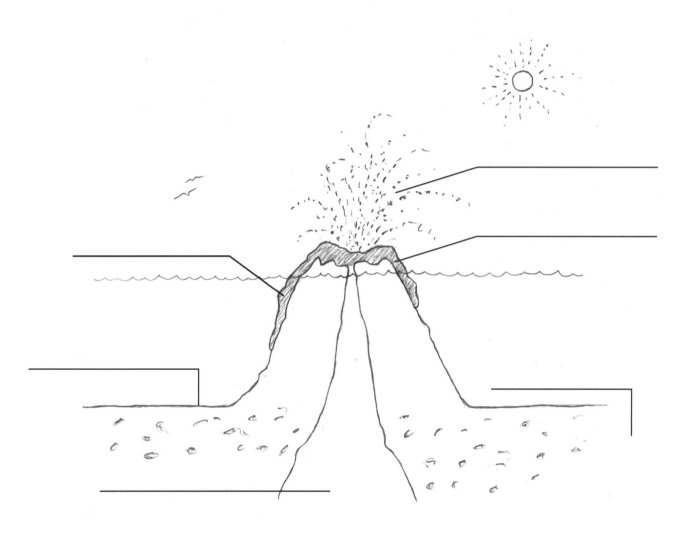

Word Bank

crust   magma chamber   ash and hot gas

ocean floor   lava

Modeling a Volcano

Supplies

2 c. clay or "clay-dough"

2 or 3 oz. bottle, approximately 3 1/2 in. tall

(If a larger bottle is used, increase the quantities of ingredients proportionally.)

1 T. baking soda

3 T. vinegar

2 drops red food color

2 drops yellow food color

8 drops blue food color

small funnel

plastic wrap

bowl or casserole dish with sides at least 4 in. high

If "clay-dough" is used, form the volcano the day before the rest of the activity. Allow 24 hours for the "clay-dough" to dry a little before continuing with Step #2.

Step #1:

Line the bowl or dish with plastic wrap for easy clean up.

Place the bottle in the center of the dish. Pat clay around the bottle and form into the shape of a volcano. Build the volcano up to the top of the bottle, but leave the "mouth" of the bottle completely open.

Pat a thin layer of clay from the base of the volcano across the bottom of the bowl or dish. This layer represents the Earth's crust, and the ocean floor.

Step #2:

Add blue food coloring to 8 cups of water. Pour the water into the dish to surround the volcano and create a "volcanic island" in the ocean.

Stick the small funnel into the top of the volcano's bottle. Pour the baking soda into the bottle and remove the funnel.

Mix vinegar and red and yellow food coloring in a mixing cup. Place the bowl or dish with the volcano into the kitchen sink.

To cause an eruption, carefully pour half of the vinegar into the bottle at the center of the "volcano." (Do not use the funnel.)

When the first "eruption" subsides, pour the remaining vinegar into the bottle for a second, lesser eruption.

When the vinegar and baking soda mix, they make a gas called carbon dioxide. This gas represents the hot gas and ash that come from inside the volcano.

The "erupting" colored liquid represents lava, flowing down the mountainside.

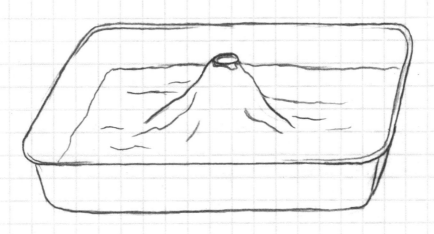

MARINE LIFE:

LIVING THINGS IN THE OCEANS

Living Things in the Oceans

Under the ocean, volcanoes rise from the Earth's crust to form islands. These islands are just part of the lands on which people, plants, and animals live. When we think of plants and animals, we often think first of those that live on land.

Yet, you remember that most of the Earth is not covered by land, but by the salty waters of seas and oceans. In these seas and oceans, God placed animals and plants that He created to live happily in salt water.

Perhaps you have a goldfish for a pet. If so, you know that your fish lives in fresh water, not salt water. Fresh water is found in creeks and rivers and lakes. It is the water that people drink.

Most fish that live in lakes and creeks and rivers are freshwater fish. If these fish are put into the salty water of oceans and seas, they will die.

The same is true for most land birds and animals and plants. Land birds, like robins and blackbirds, must have fresh water to live. Land animals like cats and dogs and deer must also have fresh water, not salt water.

Fruits and vegetables and other crops that grow in gardens and on farms are watered with freshwater rains and from freshwater rivers and lakes. Too much salt will kill all these animals and plants.

But God made fish, birds, animals, and plants that live on and in the ocean in a special way. Salt water doesn't bother them a bit! Let's find out about these special plants and animals that live on and in the oceans and seas.

Marine Plants and the Ocean Food Chain

Ocean plants, in a way, are the most important living things in the ocean. Now, that's a funny thing to say, don't you think? Scary sharks and huge whales and playful penguins seem far more interesting than ocean plants.

In fact, whether they know it or not, ocean plants are very, very important to those sharks and whales and penguins. Can you guess why?

Sharks, whales, penguins and practically every animal in the oceans could not live without ocean plants, whether they eat them or not.

This is how the system, the plan that God made for all His ocean creatures, works:

Tiny ocean plants are eaten by tiny ocean fish and animals. These little fish and animals are eaten by bigger fish, who are eaten by fish that are bigger still. Ocean birds eat the fish and animals who eat the plants. Ocean mammals eat the fish and animals who eat the plants.

And even some of the biggest whales like the Humpback, which is as long as two school buses, eat *plankton* (PLANK-tuhn), which is a kind of "thick soup" of tiny plants and animals that live in the ocean.

This "tiny plants being eaten by small fish and animals, being eaten by bigger fish and animals" is called the *food chain.*

Have you ever seen a dog chain? If you have, you know that it is made of separate pieces called links. As long as each link is strong, the whole chain is strong.

Let's imagine that you have a frisky dog who loves to run and play. Every morning and afternoon, you walk and play with your dear pet.

But when you are not playing with him, you don't want him to run away and be lost. So you fasten a long, strong chain to your dog's collar. The other

end of the chain you fasten to a stake in the ground. The long chain will hold the dog; the dog will not run away and be lost.

But what would happen if the very first link, right by the stake, broke? Your dog would run away, because the first link was broken. He might be lost forever, because of one small link.

The food chain is a little like this. Tiny ocean plants are the first links in the food chain, that link to bigger fish and bigger fish. If the plant link is broken, all the rest of the fish die.

Now do you see how important ocean plants are? Thanks be to God, many different tiny ocean plants make up that first link, so it is a very strong link. But it is also a very important one.

Algae and Plankton

Plankton is made up of tiny animals and plants that float near the surface of the ocean. This plankton is found in oceans almost all over the world. In fact, in some places, the plankton is so thick that it makes sort of thick "ocean soup" for marine animals, large and small, to slurp up!

The tiny plants in plankton are called algae (AL-jee). But not all algae are found in plankton. Other kinds of algae can grow on rocks and docks and sometimes even on marine animals like polar bears! (Algae makes polar bear fur look green.)

Another type of algae is called kelp. You will learn more about kelp in just a page or two.

Sea Grasses

While algae are not at all like land plants, sea grasses are. Like land plants, sea grasses have roots, and reach up to the sunlight to make food with their leaves. Because they must be able to reach the sunlight, sea grasses grow in shallow waters near land.

In the shallow waters near land, the sea grasses become a home for small fish and other marine animals, who eat the grasses or hide in them.

The gentle dugong, which you will learn more about later, is sometimes called a "sea cow" because it grazes on sea grasses!

Marine animals, large and small, eat plankton and algae, kelp and sea grasses. Smaller fish are eaten by larger fish, which are eaten by seals and sharks, walruses and whales in a great food chain. The first link in this food chain is ocean plants.

Kelp and a Letter from Sister Mary!

"First one done gets to read Sr. Mary's letter!" Dad grinned, pushed his plate to one side, and pulled a letter from his pocket.

"No fair! You didn't even tell us that the mail came already!" The peas rolled off Josh's fork as he tried to reach the letter in Dad's hand. "But, quick, what does she say?" he asked eagerly.

"Maybe I should finish my dinner first," Dad teased. "OK, maybe not.

"She says, 'Dear Ones; The peace of the Lord be with you all. I am just back from lunch, and thought you might like to know what was on the menu.

"'We had a delicious seaweed salad...'"

"Ewwww." Hanna made a face. "I don't think I'd like to eat seaweed."

"Too late," Mom smiled. "You eat ice cream, salad dressing, and yogurt. They are often made with agar, which comes from seaweed."

"'...full of vitamins and minerals,'" Dad read on. "'This seaweed, or kelp, is a type of algae. Mom said that you have been reading about algae in school...'"

"Hey, how did she know that?" Josh wanted to know.

"Remember her phone call last week?" Hanna reminded Josh.

"'While the tiny algae in plankton drifts about the ocean,'" Dad read on, "'kelp is usually found close to shore. But large or

small, algae is not like the plants that grow on the farm at home.

"'The corn that Dad grows has roots and leaves. These ocean plants have no roots or leaves or even flowers.

"'Instead of roots, kelp has "holdfasts," which help the plant cling to rocks. Instead of leaves, kelp has blades which act a lot like leaves.

"'Do you remember that land plants have leaves that use sunlight to help them make food for themselves? Kelp's blades do this, too. The tiny algae in plankton also use sunlight to make food for themselves.

"'Josh and Hanna, do you remember when we visited Uncle Russ and Aunt Maureen? We went to the beach and saw kelp all over the beach,'" read Dad.

"I remember!" cried Hanna. "The seaweed had 'bladders,' like thick, air-filled balloons. When we jumped on the 'bladders,' they popped. That was fun."

"Uncle Russ told us that the air-filled bladder floats right to the top of the water, holding the kelp plant up so it is on the surface," added Josh. "Up on the surface, the kelp gets plenty of sunlight, so it can make plenty of food."

"That's right," Mom said. "All that food makes kelp grow really fast! In fact, kelp grows faster than just about any other plant in the world.

"That means lots of food for marine animals to eat, and for people, too. Kelp is rich in vitamins and minerals, good things that make animals and people healthy."

"And Uncle Russ said that the thick 'beds' of kelp are also good places for small marine animals to hide," Hanna said.

"Aunt Maureen said sometimes otters sleep in the kelp beds. They even wrap themselves up in the kelp so they stay in one place while they sleep."

Dad read on, "'The next time I write, I'll try to send a copy of the salad recipe. Then maybe Mom can make seaweed salad for you at home.'"

"Or," Josh and Hanna blurted out, "not."

Dear Reader, would you like to taste some seaweed? You can find it in many grocery stores and Asian markets. The Japanese name for kelp is *nori*; in the Philippines it is called *lato*.

Ocean Plants and Land Plants
Compare and Think

In science, we compare and think about what we see. We think about ways that things are alike. We think about ways that things are different.

Ocean plants and land plants are alike in some ways. Both use sunlight to make their food and to grow.

Ocean plants and land plants are different in some ways. Ocean plants can live in salt water. Land plants cannot.

Read about these plants and look at their pictures. Compare and think. Then do the activity.

Corn is a land plant. It has roots. Corn plants use sunlight to make food. Corn needs fresh water to live. It cannot live in salt water.

Algae is an ocean plant. It does not have roots. Algae uses sunlight to make food. Ocean algae lives in salt water.

Kelp is an ocean plant. It does not have roots. Kelp uses sunlight to make food. Kelp lives in salt water.

Sea grasses are ocean plants. They have roots. They use sunlight to make food. Sea grasses live in salt water.

On the lines, print the plant names that the sentences tell about.

1. These plants are alike because they have roots.

_____

_____

2. These plants are alike because they have no roots.

_____

_____

3. These plants are alike; they use sunlight to make food.

_____

_____

4. These plants are alike because they live in salt water.

_____

_____

Marine Vertebrates

Some animals that live on land and ocean have backbones, or spines, just as you do. Animals with backbones are called *vertebrates* (VER-tuh-braytz).

Most fish are vertebrates, having skeletons inside their bodies just as you do. But God gave fish special body parts so that they could live in water. Some of these body parts are gills, fins, and tails.

If you tried to breathe under water, you would drown! But fish "breathe" underwater with the help of *gills* (GILZ), so they can breathe without drowning.

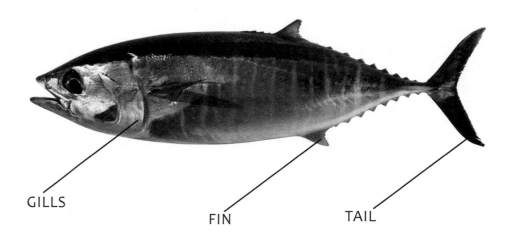

GILLS

FIN

TAIL

Instead of arms and legs, fish have fins and tails that help them turn and move quickly through their watery home. Some kinds of tuna can swim as fast as fifty miles an hour. Hang on to your sandwich!

Being fast swimmers is a big help to Bluefin Tuna,

who *migrate* (MY-grayte), or travel long distances, through the ocean each year. These big fish, which can grow to ten feet long, travel in large groups called *schools.*

You probably know that birds like geese and ducks migrate south in the fall, when the weather starts to get cold. But many fish migrate, too!

In the fall, schools of tuna move away from the colder waters in the north, to warmer waters in the south. When the weather warms, the tuna swim north again.

Another vertebrate fish is the flounder, a fish that looks like any other fish when it is small. But God gave this fish some odd characteristics.

As the fish grows, its body begins to become flat. The flounder starts to spend most of its time lying on its

Characteristics (care-ek-tuhr-ISS-ticks) is a very long word that is often used in science. Characteristics is another way of saying "ways that this plant, animal, or thing is different from other things in its group or other groups."

For example, one characteristic of people is that they have arms and legs, whereas fish have fins and tails. Feathers are characteristic of birds.

Some characteristics mark a plant or animal as being odd. It is characteristic of cats to have warm fur, but one characteristic of the Canadian Hairless cat is that it has almost no hair at all!

One very special characteristic marks people as being different from all the rest of God's Creation. All created things will someday pass away—except for people. People have eternal souls, which means that they will live forever!

And now you know what characteristics are.

side on the ocean floor. In fact, because flounders have such flat bodies and lie on the ocean floor, some people call them "doormats."

Now, a person has two eyes right in front of his face, and an ear on each side. But a fish usually has one eye on each side of its head.

When the flounder lies on his side, he has one eye looking up, with the other eye flat against the sandy ocean bottom. Poor Mr. Flounder can't see very well with only one eye looking up.

But God has a plan for Mr. Flounder. Slowly, the eye on the underside of the fish begins to move to the top! Isn't that an odd characteristic? In time, both of Mr. Flounder's eyes are on one side of his body. Now, he can look up with both eyes!

Sometimes Mr. Flounder will bury himself in the sand or mud at the bottom of the ocean so only his eyes stick out. That way he can look for food without being seen by other fish. And when he really wants to hide, he can change color so he matches the plants and rocks and sands around him!

Comparing and Contrasting Vertebrates

In science, we observe and compare. We see how things are alike. We see how things are different.

Directions:

1. Look at the pictures. What are some characteristics of the dog? For example, the dog has legs. Print the characteristics on the lines. The first one is done for you, but there are more.

Legs

_____

_____

2. What are some characteristics of the fish? Print the characteristics on the lines.

_____

_____

Look at the pictures of the dog skeleton and the fish skeleton.
How are they different? Print the differences on the lines.

3. The dog skeleton has:

_____

_____

4. The fish skeleton has:

_____

_____

Ocean Reptiles

When you think of reptiles, do you think of snakes? Snakes are found in the ocean, too!

Do you think sea snakes have gills? If you guessed "no," you are right. Fish have gills, but remember that sea snakes aren't fish. They are reptiles!

When we compare sea snakes and land snakes, we find that they are alike in some ways and different in others. Can you think of some ways that they might be alike?

Sea snakes breathe through nostrils, just like land snakes. But sea snakes can close their nostrils when they go underwater, so no water gets in. The reptiles hold their breath—sometimes for a few hours—while they swim underwater, looking for fish to eat.

Land snakes have scales to pull themselves along the ground. Sea snakes have no scales; their bodies are smooth so they can move easily through the water. Sea snakes also have tails that are shaped a little bit like a paddle, which makes the snake a strong swimmer.

Without scales, sea snakes can't move well on land; they stay always in the ocean.

Another ocean reptile is the sea turtle. These reptiles come to land to lay eggs in the warm sand, but spend all the rest of their time in the ocean.

Unlike land turtles that have legs, sea turtles have flippers, which help them swim long distances. Loggerhead Turtles migrate, swimming from Mexico, across the Pacific Ocean, to Japan and back!

Like sea snakes, sea turtles can stay underwater for several hours before coming up to breathe again. When sea turtles sleep, some lie at the top of the water with just their nostrils sticking up into the air. Then they can breathe while they sleep.

Some turtles eat plants. Others eat fish and even crabs, which they crack open with their strong jaws. The Leatherback Turtle likes jellyfish best of all.

One of the largest turtles ever found was a Leatherback that was more than eight feet long and weighed almost a ton!

Find the Right Word

Directions: Pick the correct word, then print it on the correct line.

1. I am a tiny plant found at the beginning of the food chain.

_____

2. Animals with spines are called _____.

3. This long word is a way of saying "ways that this plant, animal, or thing is different from other things in its group or other groups."

_____

4. This means "tiny plants being eaten by small fish and animals, being eaten by bigger fish and animals."

_____

5. Sea snakes don't have gills because sea snakes are

_____.

6. Fish breathe through_____ .

Word Bank

vertebrates	food chain	algae
gills	characteristics	reptiles

Ocean Birds

When an ocean reptile is compared to a land reptile, we find that these reptiles are alike in some ways and different in some ways. The same is true of land birds and ocean birds.

Both land and sea birds have feathers. Both land and sea birds are vertebrates, having backbones. But the bones and feet of land birds and sea birds are different.

Ocean birds usually have webbed feet, with skin between their "toes." These webbed feet make it easy for ocean birds to paddle across and under the water.

God gave land birds special bones that are light, so they aren't weighed down when they fly. But a few ocean birds, like penguins, don't fly at all, so they don't need light bones.

Penguins can't fly, but they can dive and swim. God gave the penguin heavier bones, which help this ocean bird dive and stay underwater as he chases fish.

Another diving and swimming ocean bird is the cormorant. Cormorants are so good at diving underwater to catch fish that Asian fishermen have used cormorants to catch fish for them. The birds wear a sort of collar and leash, and sit on the edge of the fishing boat, waiting. When the cormorant sees a fish, he dives down and gets it for the fisherman!

Perhaps you remember from last year's science lessons that the Earth we live on is divided by an imaginary line. This line, called the equator, circles the middle of the Earth.

The lands and oceans north of the equator are in the Northern Hemisphere. The lands and oceans south of the equator are in the Southern Hemisphere.

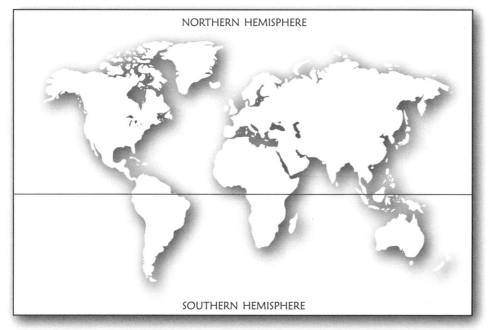

NORTHERN HEMISPHERE

EQUATOR

SOUTHERN HEMISPHERE

It is warm all year round at or close to the equator, and cold year round at the North and South Poles.

Seasons in the two hemispheres are opposite one another. When it is cold and wintery in the Northern Hemisphere, it is warm and summery in the Southern Hemisphere. When it is cold and wintery in the Southern Hemisphere, it is warm and summery in the Northern Hemisphere.

The reason this is important to ocean animals and birds is that many of them would rather live in warmer areas instead of colder areas, so they migrate.

The Arctic Tern likes to live close to the North Pole and to the South Pole. But the weather in those places is bitterly cold in the winter. So Arctic Terns migrate thousands of miles every year, back and forth between the Northern and Southern Hemispheres, spending summers in each place! Would you like to have two summers every year?

Ocean Mammals

Cows, dogs, and horses are mammals. Mammals give birth to their babies; mammal mothers feed their babies with milk from their own bodies; and mammals have hair or fur. (Mammals also have backbones, so they are vertebrates.)

You know that, unlike mammals, fish have gills so that they can "breathe" without drowning in the water around them. Mammals that live on land have no gills, for they breathe in air.

God made ocean mammals, too, like whales, dolphins, seals, and the dugong. These mammals dive and swim underwater, yet they have no gills, either. How can they breathe under water? God made a way!

Whales and dolphins breathe through nostril-like blowholes on the backs of their heads. The blowholes close when the animals dive, so no water gets in.

When a whale comes to the top of the water, the whale blows air out of its blowhole. The "blow" can be seen spraying up from the ocean like a misty fountain. (Dolphins "blow," too.)

There are several different types of

whales. Some have teeth and eat big ocean animals. Others eat plankton and krill, tiny plants and animals that live in the ocean. Instead of teeth, these whales have a sort of strainer called *baleen* (bay-LEAN).

This baleen is across the front of their mouths, with a space in the middle. Water filled with plankton and krill comes in the opening. The "soup" of plankton and krill is caught in the baleen, but the water is strained out. Just the plankton and krill are left in the whale's mouth.

Can you imagine trying to find enough tiny plants and animals to feed a huge baleen whale? Humpback Whales can grow to be sixty feet long, so you can guess how much they must eat. In one day, this whale eats enough plankton, krill, and small fish to fill two pickup trucks!

Like all whales, Humpbacks give birth to their babies. These babies, called calves, are born in the ocean. But how can the whale calf breathe?

As soon as the calf is born, the mama Humpback lifts it to the top of the water. Then she nurses the baby whale with her rich milk so it will grow a thick layer of blubber, or fat.

Humpbacks that "summer" near Alaska migrate to Hawaii to spend the winter. In the warm waters near Hawaii, they give birth to their calves. Then they migrate back to the northern Pacific for summer. Because most whales spend at least part of the year in colder parts of the ocean, thick blubber keeps them from freezing to death!

You remember that two characteristics of mammals are that they give birth to, and nurse, their babies. Do you remember another characteristic of mammals?

They have hair, or fur. Yes, since they are mammals, whales also have a tiny bit of hair. The Right Whale has "chinny whiskers." Other whales and dolphins have a few hairs around their blowholes.

Sperm whales have characteristics different from baleen whales. Sperm whales have teeth, and can open their mouths wide. They can eat big squid and sometimes even sharks!

Sperm whales can dive down deep to chase their food, and stay under water for as long as an hour without coming up for air.

The International Whaling Commission thinks that there are more than two million whales in the oceans, but whales aren't the only marine mammals.

One of these is the Killer Whale, which isn't a whale at all; it's really a dolphin!

Dolphins, too, are marine mammals. Like most animals that live in the ocean, dolphins are *carnivores* (KAHR-nuh-vohrz), or meat eaters. They dine on fish, squid, and sometimes crabs.

Dolphins like to travel in large schools with other dolphins. They play together and even work together to herd fish for dinner.

Many *marine*, or ocean-dwelling, mammals don't sleep the way people do. God made man to breathe whether he is asleep or awake; we don't have to think about breathing, we just breathe.

Unlike man, dolphins have to "decide" when to breathe. They have to stay awake all the time, or they will drown! Instead of sleeping, they rest in a different way. Some scientists think that half of a dolphin's brain sleeps while the other half stays awake.

And then there are "sea cows." When you think of cows, you probably think of animals grazing on green grass in a farmer's pasture. But the ocean has grazing animals, too.

The gentle dugong, sometimes called a sea cow, grazes on grasses in the ocean. Most of these "cows," as you might expect, are *herbivores* (UHR-buh-vohrz), or plant eaters.

These quiet creatures swim slowly through the sea grasses, the blades of grass flowing over their heads, looking a little like long hair.

With this "hair" about its head, and its large, soft eyes peeking through, some people have thought that the sea cow looked like a person in the water. Stories of mermaids probably started when someone (with a good imagination and poor eyesight) first saw a sea cow.

Dugong live in places where the ocean water is warm all year round, and can be found near the shores of the Philippines and Australia. Their close cousins, the manatees, live mostly in fresh water.

Although the gentle dugong lives in the ocean, it usually drinks fresh water. Fresh water is found in rivers and creeks that flow into the ocean, which means that the dugong aren't found too far from land.

While the dugong are found in places where it is warm year round, the walrus lives in the cold Arctic waters of the Northern Hemisphere. (There are no walruses in the Southern Hemisphere, and there are no penguins in the Northern Hemisphere.)

How does the walrus stay warm in the freezing waters of the Arctic?

God gave this marine mammal a thick layer of blubber, sometimes as much as five inches thick. When the walrus isn't swimming, he sits on "islands" of pack ice that float in the Arctic waters. How would you like to live on a giant ice cube? It's a good thing Mr. Walrus has blubber to keep him toasty warm.

Mr. Walrus has bushy whiskers, and long tusks, which can grow up to three feet long. That's a lot of tooth to brush, don't you think? But he puts the tusks to good use, as you'll soon see.

A walrus can hold his breath underwater for about thirty minutes. He can also close his nostrils tightly so no water gets in. Then Mr. Walrus dives to the ocean floor to search for his favorite meal of clams and worms and snails.

So what happens if Mr. Walrus is swimming under the ice, and can't come up for air because of the ice above him?

Simple! The walrus smashes his head against the ice to make a hole. Then he sticks his nose up through the hole to breathe. When he is sitting on top of the pack ice, he also uses his tusks to make holes to get down into the water.

Do you wonder how a walrus keeps from drowning when he sleeps in the water?

Have you ever played with an air-filled toy or ball in the water? When the toy or ball is pulled underwater, the toy pops up to the surface because of the air inside it.

The walrus has sacs under its throat that it fills with air. When the walrus sleeps, the air inside these sacs rises to the surface, as it does in your toy. The air inside these sacs, inside the walrus, holds his head above water.

Then there is the largest seal, the Elephant Seal, who

doesn't seem to sleep at all for most of the year. Marine biologists think these seals don't truly sleep, because the seals spend so much time underwater. They dive deep down to feed, come up for air, and dive again. The seals do this day and night, except for the few months of the year that they spend on land.

With that day and night feasting on squid and fish and sometimes even small sharks, these huge seals can grow to be more than twenty feet long, and weigh four tons.

But the Elephant Seal doesn't get its name because it is huge like an elephant. It gets its name from its funny, long nose.

The male seal can "blow up" its nose. He fills it full

of air so it grows longer and hangs down over its mouth. Then he uses the air in his nose to bellow so loudly that he can be heard a mile away.

Baby Elephant Seals are called pups, but they are much bigger than a dog's puppies. In fact, a newborn Elephant Seal pup is probably taller and heavier than you are! These seals are about four feet long and weigh about seventy-five pounds when they are born. (How big were you when you were born?)

We usually think of mammals as being land animals, since they don't have gills and can't "breathe" water. But our good Jesus has given each of these marine mammals, from whales to dugong to seals, everything it needs to live happily in the ocean. God plans all things well.

Bless the Lord, you whales and all creatures that move in the waters, sing praise to Him and highly exalt Him for ever.
—Daniel 3:57, RSV

Ocean Reptile, Fish, Bird, or Mammal?

Directions: Tell whether the animal is a reptile, fish, bird, or mammal. Print the word under the picture. The first one is done for you.

mammal

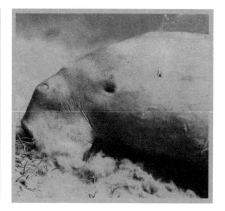

Marine Invertebrates

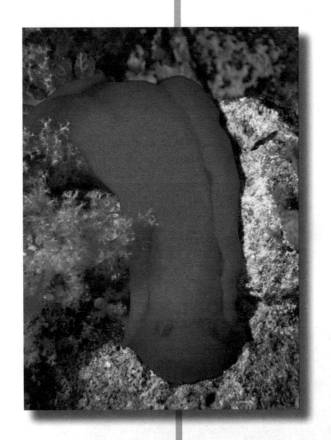

Animals without backbones are called *invertebrates* (inn-VUHR-tuh-braytz). The oceans are filled with thousands of different kinds of invertebrates like sea slugs, clams, squid, and starfish.

Do you think slugs are pretty? Sea slugs are beautiful! They come in almost every color you can imagine. Some are even polka-dotted! The "Spanish Dancer" sea slug has a colorful red "skirt" that seems to swirl like the skirts of a Spanish dancer.

Sea slugs mostly eat ocean plants, including dead plant "garbage." Sea slugs help keep the ocean clean by eating this "ocean trash."

Sea slugs, like land slugs, move too slowly to get away from other animals that like to eat them. Can you guess how God protects these ocean animals?

Sea slugs eat colorful plants; some take on the color of the plants they eat. If the plant is red, the sea slug turns red. If the plant is green, the sea slug turns green. Since the sea slug matches the plants that he eats, he can feast without being seen.

Sea slugs belong to a group of ocean animals called *mollusks* (MALL-uhsks), which we will learn more about later.

Another ocean invertebrate is the crab. Like sea slugs that "clean up" the oceans, crabs are also "ocean trashmen" who eat dead ocean animals. Most crabs are omnivores, who eat plants, fish, and other crabs, too.

Instead of an "inside skeleton," the crab has an *exoskeleton* (ECKS-oh-skell-uh-tuhn), a kind of shell that covers the outside of its body.

With their ten legs, crabs walk sideways. Their front legs are two big pinching claws that help them catch food, and fight off other animals who want to eat them.

Sometimes crabs can lose a leg when they are fighting another animal. One of the interesting characteristics of crabs is that they can grow a new leg to replace the one they have lost!

There are about six thousand different kinds of crabs in the ocean. One that you might not want to meet is the Great Japanese Spider Crab, which can live to be one hundred years old, and grow to twelve feet wide from the end of one front claw to the end of the other.

Another, smaller, invertebrate is the shrimp. Like crab, shrimp have an exoskeleton and ten legs. But shrimp are much better swimmers than crabs, and move easily through the water.

Do you like to eat shrimp? So do starfish, whales, dolphins, and lots of other, bigger ocean animals! And can you guess what shrimp eat? They eat even tinier algae and plankton.

Yet another marine invertebrate is the starfish. When you think of starfish, do you think of the kind with five arms, that looks most like a star? Did you know that some kinds of starfish have as many as fifty arms? And, like crabs, if a starfish loses a leg, he can grow another one in its place.

The underside of a starfish's legs are covered with tiny "suction cups." When the starfish finds a clam to eat, he gives it a big "hug," wrapping his legs around the clam. The "suction cups" hold the clam and slowly pull open its shell. Then the starfish eats the clam inside.

Jellyfish and coral are invertebrates, too. Many people think that the bright, colorful coral are plants, but they are not. Coral are animals, too. Jellyfish and coral are close relatives, but have very different characteristics.

Jellyfish are carnivores; they eat small fish and other ocean animals. Jellyfish have soft bodies, and "breathe" through their skins!

Instead of fins, these ocean animals have thin arms and tentacles (TEHN-tuh-kuhlz) that help them catch and eat food. (Most jellyfish sting, so you would not want to try to catch one.)

Jellyfish swim about the ocean catching food, but coral are tiny animals that stay in one place. They make a hard shell around their tiny bodies, to keep them safe.

Coral make their hard-shelled "homes" on top of the empty shells of coral that lived there before them. When those coral die, more coral build on top of the empty shells. After a time, layers and layers and layers of old coral shells grow into a sort of giant underwater "castle" called a *reef*, with living coral at the top.

These giant "underwater castles" are home not only to coral, but also to huge numbers of fish, who feed as they dart in and out of their beautiful coral home.

Do you wonder how coral catch food, if they are forever "glued" in one place? Like the jellyfish, coral have tentacles, too. The tentacles catch tiny sea animals as they float past the coral's safe home.

Crabs, starfish, jellyfish, and coral are all invertebrates of the ocean. And now, we will finally learn about mollusks!

Mollusks

Mollusks are invertebrates, too. When people think of mollusks, they often think of shellfish with soft bodies inside and hard shells outside, like clams and oysters. But not all mollusks have shells!

The squid and the octopus are mollusks, too. Both octopus and squid have eight arms with rows of "suction-cups" for grabbing and holding onto rocks and also food.

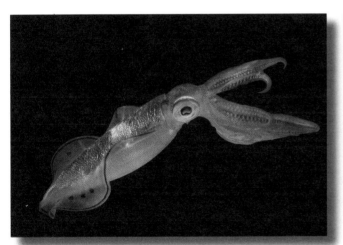

Squid also have tentacles that they use to snatch other animals. Unlike their arms, "suction cups" are found only at the very end of a squid's tentacles.

Since an octopus has no tail or fins, you might wonder how it can move quickly enough to get away from other animals that want to eat it. The octopus can squirt water from its body, which makes the octopus shoot off in the opposite direction. Squid can speed away like this, too.

And how else do these soft-bodied mollusks protect themselves, besides speeding away?

Both squid and octopus have a type of "ink" that they can squirt into the water around them. The water turns cloudy and dark, so other animals can't see the squid or octopus. Hidden by the cloud of ink, the squid and octopus slip safely away.

Have you ever seen a baby get red in the face when it is in an angry mood? Squid and octopus can change color when they are "moody," too. Like the flounder, they can also change color when they want to hide.

Clams are mollusks with shells, and are a favorite food of sea gulls. Many clams can "burrow" into the sand to stay safe from animals that want to have them for lunch, but other clams are protected mostly by their shells. Of course, the shells are no match for a hungry walrus, who likes clams as much as sea gulls do.

Most clams are only a few inches long, but some are so large that a sea gull couldn't possibly pick one up. A giant clam, the Tridacna Maxima, can grow to be 4 feet long. That would make a lot of clam chowder!

Have you ever seen a pearl necklace or ring? Pearls are made when a tiny piece of sand slips inside a mollusk's shell. Like a painful rock in your shoe, the sharp sand pokes into the soft body of the mollusk.

Now, you have hands and fingers, which make it easy to remove the rock from your shoe. But a mollusk has no arms, hands or fingers. It cannot remove the sharp sand that is inside its shell. What's a mollusk to do?

The mollusk coats the sharp sand with a special material so the sand becomes smoother. After a time, the material gets thicker and thicker, making a beautiful pearl around the tiny piece of sand. Most pearls come from oysters, but sometimes pearls are found in clams and other mollusks, too.

Comparing Vertebrates and Invertebrates in Your Soup

Fish are vertebrates; they have backbones. Shrimp, crabs, and clams are invertebrates. They have no backbones.

This soup recipe contains all of these ocean animals. As you help make this soup, observe these very different animals. Use the worksheet on page 142 to tell how they are the same, and how they are different.

Note: This soup is one of many cioppino variations; it is a hearty "Friday" fish stew, meant to be eaten with both spoon and fingers. Enjoy with a crusty french bread.

Directions:

Examine the fish. Note scales (if they haven't been removed), fins, tail, and gills.

Scale fish, if necessary; remove head. Poach fish in 1 cup of water; cool and save water.

Ingredients

10 clams, in shell (oysters may be substituted)

1 cooked crab, in shell

1 pound cooked shrimp, in shell

1 raw, cleaned fish of choice, preferably with head, fins, and tail

Examine the shrimp. Do they have backbones, or an exoskeleton? Remove shells and devein; set shrimp aside in large pot.

Examine the clams. Are they vertebrates, or invertebrates? If clams are uncooked, steam in 1 cup of water until they open. Set aside on plate; save water.

Examine the crab. Is it a vertebrate or an invertebrate? How many legs does it have? How many claws? Are the claws the same size? (If one claw is larger than the other, it is possible that the crab lost the first claw and grew another.)

Remove the top shell from the crab. Pull meat from the body and set in pot with the shrimp. Remove legs and claws. Put legs and claws in pot with the shrimp.

When the fish is cool, remove the flesh and put it in the pot with the shrimp. Add water from poaching to the pot. Examine the fish skeleton. Is the fish a vertebrate or an invertebrate?

Add to seafood in pot:
  2 one-pound cans of crushed tomatoes

In separate saucepan, sauté for five minutes:
  3 T. olive oil
  1 chopped onion
  3 garlic cloves, chopped fine
  1 green pepper, chopped
  1 tsp. salt
  1/4 tsp. pepper

All optional:
  spices of your choice, or:
  dash of dried thyme
  1 bay leaf
  1/2 c. fresh parsley, chopped
  1 c. red or white wine

Now put sauteed vegetables and clam stock (if clams were already cooked when purchased, add 1 c. water instead) in the large pot with the seafood. Bring to a boil, then simmer for 20 minutes.

Now add clams to the pot. Return to boil, then simmer for 5 minutes more.

Serve with french bread and plenty of napkins.

WORKSHEET: COMPARING VERTEBRATES AND INVERTEBRATES IN YOUR SOUP

Fish are vertebrates; they have backbones. Shrimp, crabs, and clams are invertebrates. They have no backbones. Look carefully at these animals as you make your soup.

1. In what ways are the clams different from the shrimp?

_____

_____

_____

2. In what ways are the shrimp different from the crabs?

_____

_____

_____

3. How is the fish different from the crabs, clams, and shrimp?

_____

_____

_____

Vertebrate or Invertebrate?

You remember that vertebrates have spines, or backbones. Invertebrates have no backbones. Some have exoskeletons, or shells on the outside of their bodies. Other invertebrates have neither exoskeletons nor spines.

Directions: Tell whether the animal is a vertebrate or an invertebrate. Circle the correct word under the picture. The first one is done for you.

vertebrate (invertebrate)

vertebrate   invertebrate

vertebrate   invertebrate

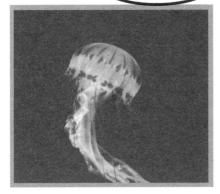
vertebrate   invertebrate

vertebrate   invertebrate

vertebrate   invertebrate

vertebrate   invertebrate

vertebrate   invertebrate

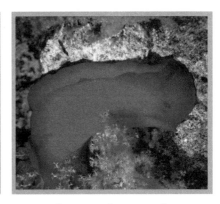
vertebrate   invertebrate

Deep in the Ocean

You know that there are tall mountains and low valleys on land. But under the oceans, there are tall mountains that rise into volcanic islands, and low valleys as well.

Where land meets the ocean, the water is shallow. Bright sunlight can shine through the shallow water on colorful fish that flit about below. Ocean plants like kelp grow and float along the shoreline.

In other places, deep underwater "valleys" lie far below the ocean's surface. In these ocean "valleys," the water is so deep that no light from the sun can reach through the water.

With no sunlight to help them make food, plants cannot grow. It is dark and cold in the deepest parts of the Earth's oceans.

How can anything live in these dark places, where the water is close to freezing all year round?

God made a way!

Deep under the ocean, volcanoes erupt. Near these volcanoes are cracks in the ocean floor. Cold ocean water flows down into these cracks, so close to the

fiery hot magma under the ocean floor.

In these fiery cracks under the ocean floor, the water becomes very hot. Then this heated water shoots up, like a fountain of hot water! These cracks, from which heated water shoots up, are called *vents*.

Marine biologists, or scientists who study marine life, used to think that nothing could live at the dark, cold bottom of the ocean. But they didn't know about ocean vents! (Can you guess Who knew about vents all along?)

In the past several years, using very special submarines, these scientists have made many trips to the bottom of the oceans. They have been surprised to find clams, crabs, fish, worms, and many other animals living in the darkest, deepest parts of the ocean.

These deep sea creatures are very different, however, from the marine animals that live in shallower parts of the ocean. Some of these creatures live in the hot water near the vents. Others live in the cold water away from vents. But each animal has characteristics that help it live quite happily in the deepest parts of the ocean.

Now remember that there is no sunlight for plants to grow here. What happens to that first link in the food chain? How can these animals live if the first link in the chain is missing?

God made a way! (Did you know I was going to say that?)

Many of these creatures, like deep sea clams, live on  "*marine snow,*" which is tiny pieces of dead fish, plankton, and plants that drift like snow to the bottom of the ocean.

Others feed on "*whale falls,*" or dead whales that have sunk to the bottom of the ocean. Now, you know how big whales are; it is thought that one "whale fall" has as much food as a thousand years of "marine snow."

And one kind of tubeworm lives and feeds on nothing but whale bones!

Then there is the Galatheid Crab, or Squat Lobster. How would you like to sit down to a dinner of dead wood? If you were a Galatheid, you'd dig right in! This odd little deep sea creature feeds on wood that sinks to the ocean floor in "*wood falls*."

Isn't God's creation amazing?

And there's more!

There are deep sea fish that catch and eat other fish. But how can they tell where the other fish are in the dark? If a hungry fish can't see other fish, how can it chase and catch them? (Can you say it before I do?)

God made a way!

An anglerfish has a built-in "fishing pole" growing above its head. The "fishing pole" even has a glowing light on the end. In the black darkness, smaller fish

see the light and think it is something yummy to eat. When the little fish takes a bite of the light, the anglerfish flips the end of his "fishing pole" into his mouth, along with his catch.

Another anglerfish, the Wolftrap Angler, doesn't even need a "fishing pole." He has a "lighted lure" just inside his mouth. If he is hungry, all he needs to do is open wide! When a smaller fish swims to the light, the Wolftrap just shuts his mouth and enjoys his dinner.

Now, would you like to be a marine biologist someday, and maybe discover yet more of God's amazing deep sea creatures?

...He stilled the great deep and planted islands in it.
Those who sail the sea tell of its dangers, and we marvel at what we hear.
For in it are strange and marvelous works, all kinds of living things, and huge creatures of the sea.
—*Sirach 43:23-25, RSV*

Measuring Up

Supplies

backyard

long measuring tape

index cards

something to weight the index cards down to keep them from blowing away

Before you go outside, write the name and length of each animal on two index cards, one animal per card.

In your backyard, lay the first card on the ground and weight it with a rock. Measure the length of the animal, starting from the first card, and ending with the placement of the second card. For example, the Tridacna Maxima would have 4 feet between the two cards.

Sea slug: 3 inches (Because this animal is so small, you may use one card.)

Tridacna Maxima clam: 4 feet

Elephant Seal pup at birth: 4 feet

Sea Turtle: 8 ft.

Walrus: 10 feet

Tuna: 10 feet

Great Japanese Spider Crab: 12 feet from claw tip to claw tip

Elephant Seal, male: 20 feet long

Humpback Whale: 60 feet

And how tall are *you*?

Deep-Sea Words

Directions:

Circle the word that fits the blank. The first one is done for you.

1. Some deep sea marine animals eat wood that falls to the bottom. This is called a:

a. Christmas tree   (b. wood fall)   c. crab

2. Other marine creatures eat tiny pieces of dead fish, plankton, and plants that drift to the bottom as:

a. raindrops   b. fish   c. marine snow

3. Some marine creatures eat dead whales that have fallen to the ocean floor. This is called a:

a. whale fall   b. marine snow   c. wood fall

4. A scientist who studies plants and animals in the oceans is called a:

a. pirate   b. marine biologist   c. student

5. Cracks in the ocean floor from which heated water shoots up are called:

a. vents   b. faucets   c. volcanoes

Answer Key

6

Tools at Work

Tools are things that make work easier.

Saws, scissors, and knives are used for cutting. Saws, scissors, and knives are tools that make work easier.

If you did not have a shovel, how would you dig a hole? If you did not have a broom, how would you sweep crumbs from the floor?

Shovels and brooms are tools that make work easier.

Directions: Circle the things that are tools.

11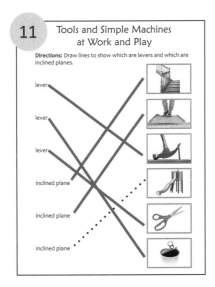

Tools and Simple Machines at Work and Play

Directions: Draw lines to show which are levers and which are inclined planes.

lever
lever
lever
inclined plane
inclined plane
inclined plane

21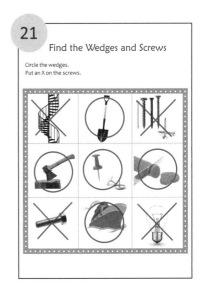

Find the Wedges and Screws

Circle the wedges.
Put an X on the screws.

32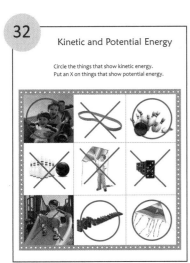

Kinetic and Potential Energy

Circle the things that show kinetic energy.
Put an X on things that show potential energy.

43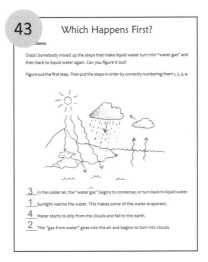

Which Happens First?

Oops! Somebody mixed up the steps that make liquid water turn into "water gas" and then back to liquid water again. Can you figure it out?

Figure out the first step. Then put the steps in order by correctly numbering them 1, 2, 3, 4.

3 In the colder air, the "water gas" begins to condense, or turn back to liquid water.

1 Sunlight warms the water. This makes some of the water evaporate.

4 Water starts to drip from the clouds and fall to the earth.

2 This "gas from water" goes into the air and begins to turn into clouds.

55

Find the Natural Resources

God created our natural resources. Man uses and makes things from these natural resources, but man cannot make the natural resources themselves.

Circle the natural resources that God created.

62

"Dig Up" the Correct Word
1. dirt
2. sand
3. clay
4. loam
5. eroded
6. repair

72

Layers of the Earth
1. core
2. crust
3. mantle

80

"Matching" Rocks
1. limestone
2. metamorphic
3. igneous
4. magma
5. pumice
6. sandstone

Land-building Volcanoes

Use words from the Word Bank to label the picture.
One word is used twice.
When you finish the labels, color the picture!

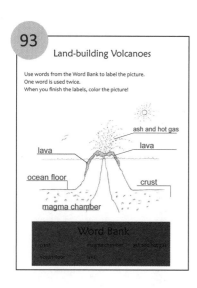

ash and hot gas

lava | lava

ocean floor | crust

magma chamber

Word Bank

crust | magma chamber | ash and hot gas
ocean floor | lava

Ocean Plants and Land Plants

1. corn, sea grasses
2. algae, kelp
3. corn, algae, kelp, sea grasses
4. algae, kelp, sea grasses

Comparing and Contrasting Vertebrates

Answers will vary; some possibilities include:
1. legs, tail, fur, nose
2. tail, scales, fins, gills
3. leg, tail, ribs, skull, spine
4. spine, skull

Find the Right Word

1. algae
2. vertebrates
3. characteristics
4. food chain
5. reptiles
6. gills

Reptile, Fish, Bird, or Mammal?

Directions: Tell whether the animal is a reptile, fish, bird, or mammal. Print the word under the picture. The first one is done for you.

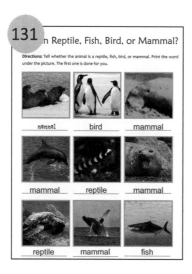

mammal | bird | mammal

mammal | reptile | mammal

reptile | mammal | fish

Comparing Vertebrates & Invertebrates

Answers will vary; some possibilities include:

1. Clams have 2 shells and no legs; shrimp have an exoskeleton with legs.
2. Shrimp have thinner shells, no claws, and a tail.
3. The fish has a spine, bones, scales, and fins.

The fish has a different type of gills.

Vertebrate or Invertebrate?

You remember that vertebrates have spines, or backbones. Invertebrates have no backbones. Some have exoskeletons, or shells on the outside of their bodies. Other invertebrates have neither exoskeletons nor spines.

Directions: Tell whether the animal is a vertebrate or an invertebrate. Circle the correct word under the picture. The first one is done for you.

vertebrate (invertebrate) | vertebrate (invertebrate) | vertebrate (invertebrate)

vertebrate (invertebrate) | vertebrate (invertebrate) | vertebrate (invertebrate)

(vertebrate) invertebrate | (vertebrate) invertebrate | vertebrate (invertebrate)

Deep-Sea Words

1. b
2. c
3. a
4. b
5. a

Distributed by

Catholic Heritage Curricula

P.O. Box 579090, Modesto, California 95357

To request a free catalog, call toll-free: 1-800-490-7713
Or visit online: *www.chcweb.com*

If your child enjoyed and benefited from this book, perhaps you would also enjoy some of CHC's other homeschooling materials, whether for extra practice outside of school, homeschooling, or character development.

Other titles by Nancy Nicholson:

I Can Find Letter Sounds

Little Folks' Letter Practice

Little Stories for Little Folks: Catholic Phonics Readers

What Do You Like to Do... Easy Reader

Devotional Stories for Little Folks

My Catholic Speller Series

Catholic Heritage Handwriting Series

Behold and See 1: On the Farm with Josh and Hanna

I Can Find Numbers and Shapes

Little Folks' Number Practice

Bigger Stories for Little Folks

What Can You Do... Easy Reader

Devotional Stories for Little Folks, Too

Language of God Series

High School of Your Dreams

Onions in My Boots